I0569042

The Lady In Waiting

THE SINGLE LADY'S GUIDE TO PREPARING FOR KINGDOM MARRIAGE

Deborah Idowu-Asufi

The Lady In Waiting
The Single Lady's Guide to Preparing for Kingdom Marriage

Copyright © 2024 Deborah Idowu-Asufi

All rights reserved. No part of this publication may be reproduced, distributed, or transmitted in any form or by any means, including photocopying, recording, or other electronic or mechanical means without proper written permission of the author or publisher, except in the case of brief quotations embodied in critical reviews and certain other noncommercial uses permitted by copyright law.

Paperback ISBN: 978-1-963732-12-2
Hardcover ISBN: 978-1-963732-13-9

Scripture quotations marked AMPC taken from the Amplified® Bible (AMPC), Copyright © 1954, 1958, 1962, 1964, 1965, 1987 by The Lockman Foundation. Used by permission. lockman.org.

Scripture quotations marked NASB are taken from the NASB® New American Standard Bible®, Copyright © 1960, 1971, 1977, 1995, 2020 by The Lockman Foundation. Used by permission. All rights reserved. lockman.org.

Scripture quotations marked NIV are taken from THE HOLY BIBLE, NEW INTERNATIONAL VERSION®, NIV® Copyright © 1973, 1978, 1984, 2011 by Biblica, Inc.® Used by permission. All rights reserved worldwide.

Scripture marked NKJV is taken from the New King James Version®. Copyright © 1982 by Thomas Nelson. Used by permission. All rights reserved.

Scripture quotations marked NLT are taken from the Holy Bible, New Living Translation, copyright © 1996, 2004, 2015 by Tyndale House Foundation. Used by permission of Tyndale House Publishers, Inc., Carol Stream, Illinois 60188. All rights reserved.

Scripture quotations marked TPT are from The Passion Translation®. Copyright © 2017, 2018, 2020 by Passion & Fire Ministries, Inc. Used by permission. All rights reserved. ThePassionTranslation.com.

The names used in this book have been changed to protect the privacy of the individuals. However, every story is real, and I hope they inspire you to learn, grow, and do better.

Published By

The Publishing Pad
www.thepublishingpad.com

Dedication

I have written this book as a married woman who has journeyed through seasons of pain, grief, loss, restoration, and joy. I am deeply thankful for the structures built into me in my single days and for the support system that I could lean on when the storm came and the floods shook my building to its very foundations. By the grace of God, I am still standing—and will continue to stand.

I dedicate this book to you, dear lady in waiting, as you learn to lean into the divine and walk with the King of Kings as your Father.

As you are reminded of His promises to you and the assurance of His unwavering love, I pray you find Him, find yourself, and find love in the pages of this book.

I love you, and I pray you find answers through the vulnerability, experiences, testimonies, and victories shared in this book—mine and those of countless other women.

Introduction

Marriage is such a beautiful journey when done right. Much like a stool with solid legs that remains standing even under a heavy load, the marriage institution requires a sturdy foundation of preparation and self-awareness. When a woman prepares herself thoroughly, she understands her self-worth and refuses to settle for anything less than the best for herself.

Unfortunately, many ladies get married without first discovering the reason for their existence. When they later become self-aware and understand their life's purpose, they experience unimaginable conflict with their spouses because each person's intentions, values, and purpose no longer align with those of the other. This is one of the reasons I have written this book: to help single ladies discover themselves and address critical questions that'll help them choose the right life partner.

Divorce is real, and so is the pain of a cheating spouse. Many ladies have met an untimely death due to bad marriages. Yet every week, many more unprepared ladies walk down the aisle unaware of what they are getting into . . . this is like a disaster waiting to happen. Far too often, we hear a married sister say, "I didn't know any better when I married him." This has got to stop, and I believe that this is why you are reading this book—to know better and save yourself from the stress and pain of choosing the wrong partner.

We all act based on our level of knowledge; that is why the Bible says in Hosea 4:6 (NKJV), "My people are destroyed for lack of knowledge." Your choices and outcomes are shaped by what you know. If you come from a single-parent family, are an orphan, witnessed your parents go through a painful divorce, or watched your parents suffer from addictions or unhealed trauma, or whatever the case may be for you that is not pleasant, you may want a better experience for yourself and your children. But without the right knowledge and the application of this knowledge, you may end up making the same mistakes your parents did. This is the second reason for this book: to help you identify and address deep-rooted issues that can hinder your happiness in marriage.

When done right, marriage can feel like heaven on earth. It offers you the right support system, a friend, a prayer partner—an all-in-one package. This is the kind of marriage you should desire and walk towards, because it is attainable. I have experienced it and continue to do so, and I will show you how.

Even if you come from a stable family and witnessed zero drama in your parents' marriage, you still need this book. The updated and relatable tools inside will provide you with a "cutting edge," helping you maximize and amplify your strengths so you can build on a great foundation to offer yourself and your children an even better family life.

For those who are already married, this book will open your eyes to areas you probably didn't even know needed to be addressed. Applying the insights in this book can lead you to the heaven-on-earth marriage you always desired. It is actually possible. You don't need to feel bad and say, "Oh . . . I am not getting all the support I need/want from my spouse." Through this book, you will learn to understand yourself, understand the spouse you are married to, and learn to seek support from the people God has placed in your life.

To the divorced single lady, I see you! I see your desire to find love again, and I know that by reading this book, you will arm yourself with the right information to realign with your purpose and connect with the man who is right for you.

For the single woman who has experienced loss, you will smile again. Whether you choose to remarry or not, you are holding a treasure that will mark you positively as you navigate this season of your life. Regardless of your age, I want you to know you are beautiful, valuable, and special, and I know this book will change your life forever in meaningful ways.

Fathers and brothers may be intrigued about the contents of this book. I assure you, you will find interesting principles and information that will open your eyes to how women think. This book will also show men and women the best way to approach and support the single women in their lives as they navigate this season of life, maximize it, and stay aligned to their God-given purpose.

To the church leader, therapist, or counselor, this book is a powerful tool to help your clients and church members discover their purpose, heal from past wounds, and live their best lives.

As a certified life coach, I have been privileged to counsel many people, some of whose stories you will read in this book. My sole aim is to equip every woman with the right knowledge and support to become the best version of themselves.

I am excited because your life is about to change for the better. Let's jump right into chapter one!

CHAPTER 1
Abuse, Trauma, and Emotional Wounds

Someone once said that all families are dysfunctional, but some are more dysfunctional than others. That was the case with Marilyn. Marilyn adored her mom and was the apple of her father's eye. Yet it was not uncommon to hear her parents yelling at each other during disagreements. As a teenager, she noticed that her dad would stay away from home for days at a time. When she asked about it, her mom explained that he had to work out of state. Marilyn observed that her mom seemed happier when her dad was away but that her mood would suddenly turn sober the moment he returned, even if it was only for a few days.

As time went on, her dad came home less often, and even when he returned, he never spent more than a day there before returning to what had become his main base. This meant fewer arguments and raised voices in Marilyn's home. Still, Marilyn often saw her mom crying herself to sleep. When she asked why, her mom would say she had to numb her emotions just to stay married to her husband because her husband always hurt her and she was tired of crying with zero change on his part. But Marilyn couldn't reconcile her mom's version of her dad with her own experiences. She believed her life was beautiful. Her dad was very generous, and her friends and anyone who met him felt really comfortable around him.

Marilyn continued to live in her bubble until the day she went to visit her dad out of state. She found that he would stay up late talking sweet nothings to another woman he called "baby." This new revelation about her dad broke her, so she confronted him. He claimed there was nothing wrong with what he was doing. In fact, he rebuked Marilyn for eavesdropping on his late-night conversations. All week, he would spend some days at his girlfriend's house or invite her over to his house, and then on Sunday he would go to church and sing the congregational hymns loudly and boldly. When it was time to give, her dad would contribute a huge percentage to church financial projects, and the pastor would call him Brother John. He was respected in the church, but his two-faced lifestyle broke Marilyn within.

She could no longer stand this version of her dad and had to return home, where she shared her observations with her mom, who admitted that she was aware of the affair. Her mom explained that the affair was the reason she stopped visiting her husband because every visit broke her heart. Her mom's admission shocked Marilyn, who silently vowed that no man would take her for granted or treat her in such a despicable way in marriage.

In her search for love and not wanting to be taken for granted, Marilyn fell into the hands of men who abused her emotionally and sexually. They took from her and gave her nothing in return. Now she believes all men are scum and there are no genuine men out there, especially men who claim to know God.

Now comes a gentleman genuinely interested in investing in a relationship with Marilyn. They marry, and he does everything possible to show her how much he loves her, but because of her past, Marilyn continues to frustrate his efforts. The marriage suffers because she hasn't healed from the hurts of her past. She is judging her husband for the sins of her father.

Does this story sound familiar? On the outside, this family looked cool, calm, and collected, but on the inside, there was the pain of betrayal, unfaithfulness, anger, and bitter words exchanged. Many of us are coming from a similar place of hurt and betrayal.

If women like Marilyn do not properly address these painful emotions and emotional wounds before marriage, chances are that every act of their spouses will be looked at with scrutiny and mistrust. Any error on the spouse's part will be met with a terrifying response that has the potential to break that relationship. If these traumas aren't dealt with, she will either destroy her marriage with her own hands or, just like Marilyn's mother, numb herself to her emotions to prevent herself from getting hurt. That's because this is all she knows. Remember that we cannot give what we don't have. We won't be able to resolve conflicts amicably if we never learned how. Period.

A lot of us grew up learning to find coping mechanisms to deal with unpleasant situations, even to the detriment of our health. We weren't taught to address issues, or maybe we were, but we think it's safer and better to just run. But for how long would you run? How long would you numb yourself and endure that unsatisfactory situation?

What if there is a solution to be happy? Wouldn't you rather try?

You can be happy again. There is indeed a solution, and the first step to this transformation is awareness. You must come to the place where you are aware and acknowledge that you have experienced trauma, abuse, or emotional wounds. That self-awareness is the beginning of your transformation.

Let's briefly define these terms for better understanding:

Abuse is when a person is treated with cruelty or violence, especially when it happens regularly or repeatedly.

Trauma is a deeply distressing or disturbing experience that affects one's outlook on life.

Emotional wounds are the mental and psychological pain caused by difficult, traumatic, or negative experiences. This pain goes on and on for weeks, months, years. Just like physical wounds on the body, emotional wounds, if left untreated, begin to manifest in the body as physical pain from the head to the feet. Emotional wounds often give rise to addictions.

Observe what the book of Proverbs 18:14 (TPT) says: "The will to live sustains you when you're sick, but depression crushes courage and leaves you unable to cope."

Many people are walking around with unhealed trauma, abuse, and emotional wounds as a result of events that took place in their past. I want you to ask yourself these questions and answer them genuinely (this is a no-judgement zone):

- Do you abuse others, or have you been called an abuser in the past?
- Do you constantly experience fear?
- Do you constantly feel angry, neglected, ashamed, or overly sensitive?
- Do you experience deep feelings of loneliness, abandonment, etc.?

If you answered yes to any of these questions, then you have some unprocessed trauma to deal with. I once heard a story about a woman with completely bent knees who walked with crutches. One day she met an intuitive man, and the first thing he said to her was, "Ma'am, would you be willing to release the people you are bitter against?" This lady burst into tears, repeatedly saying how people had hurt her and she couldn't bring herself to forgive them. At the end of the session, she summoned the courage to let go, and a week later, her legs straightened. She no longer needed crutches to walk.

Wow! How deadly these unhealed traumas can be—and yet forgiveness has real power. Many of us are like this woman, carrying with us loads of unprocessed trauma. Then we make the mistake of getting into marriage without addressing these internal issues. What this does is it affects our choice of a partner and places undue pressure on another human being to make us happy. And the truth is that happiness must first come from within.

I have learned that happiness is a choice, and you are the person who will decide to be happy. No matter what is going on around you, you can choose to be happy, but this will not happen if you haven't healed yet from the past. Because when you have not healed from this inner turmoil, you will constantly feel like a victim. When you are broken on the inside, you will find that you are attracted to the wrong people—people who end up taking advantage of your vulnerability.

Figure 1 (below) is a body map of stored emotions manifesting as pain in the body. This map shows how unhealed trauma and emotional wounds can affect your body and your health negatively. For instance, the heart is a place where joy and love reside, so when people begin to experience pain in the heart, it may simply mean there is an unhealed emotional wound.

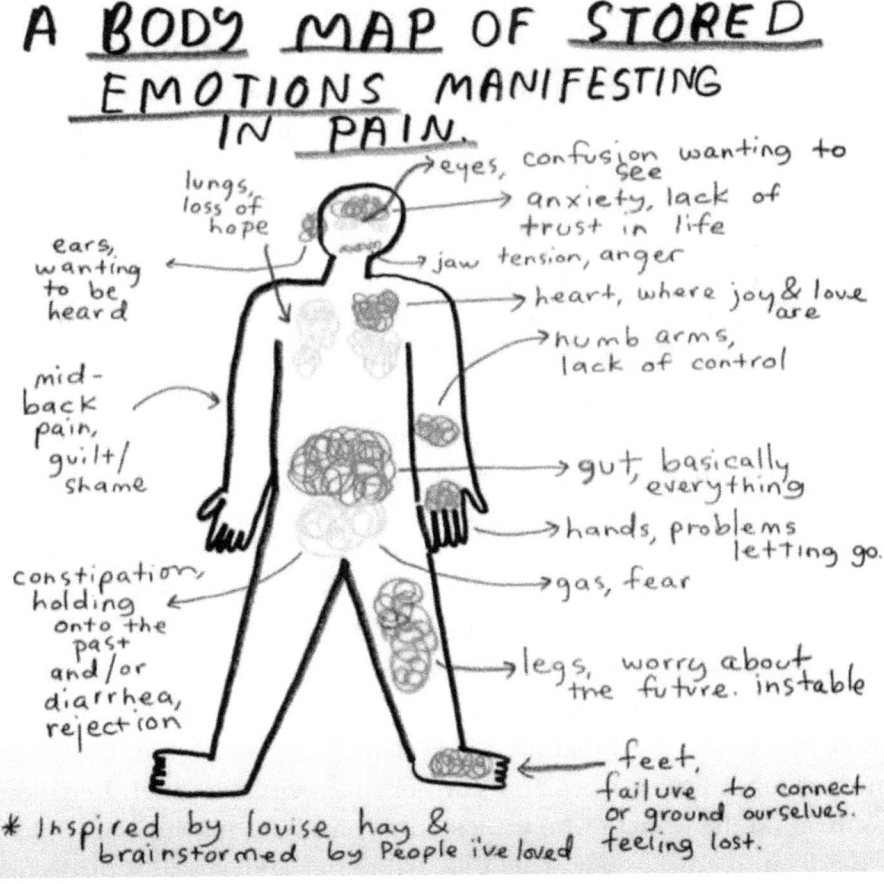

Figure 1. This map shows where unresolved negative emotions can manifest as pain in the body.

It shows what happens when we continue life without first treating the wounds that we have encountered on our journeys. If you have unaddressed and unhealed abuse and trauma, the unhealed wound creates a fertile environment for the roots of addiction to flourish. Psalm 34:18

(TPT) says: "The Lord is close to all whose hearts are crushed by pain, and he is always ready to restore the repentant one." You are deeply loved by a great God who wants you to heal so you can truly live the life He intended for you.

Jane was raped as a child but never processed or healed from this wound. As she became a teenager, she got involved with multiple sexual partners. She believed that her body was what made her desirable. She knew these men did not love her, but she kept giving her body to them and hoping that one day they would love her.

This is the story of many women.

I met a lady whom I will call Julia. Julia was a successful medical doctor who was well loved by her patients and clients, but her marriage wasn't as successful as her career. At the time I met her, she was already separated from her husband. Professionally, she was on top of her game, but emotionally and psychologically, she was a wreck. Curious to know how this happened, I asked her if she had always been like this as a child—scared, unsure of herself, living in her past. She thought about this for a bit before responding no.

"So, what was childhood like?" I asked her. She smiled and shared that she had happy, sweet, beautiful memories until she and her siblings became adolescents and her dad had to travel a lot. Her mom was also busy with furthering her education, leaving her and her siblings in the care of relatives. She recalled one time when her father's stepsister beat her so hard that her left eyeball shifted backward. When her mom returned from work and saw her, she wept. Although her mom confronted the woman who inflicted this harm on this little girl, Julia's self-esteem died that day. The abuse stole her audacity and made her unsure of herself.

You see, the seeds of problems many people face as adults or in their marriages are often planted as abuse and trauma in their childhood or unmarried years because the enemy understands the law of sowing and reaping. He sows these seeds and allows them to take root, and when allowed to grow unchecked, they can influence the marriage decision and other aspects of one's life.

A lot of issues people have in their marriages started out as seeds of events or actions sowed in their past. And because we are human, our common reaction, our way of protecting ourselves from the hurt, is to feel victimized and to either lash out or withdraw.

The Bible says in 2 Timothy 1:7 (NLT): "For God has not given us a spirit of fear and timidity, but of power, love, and self-discipline." So, if you operate in fear or are timid, you need to begin to question where that fear or timidity is coming from. It's definitely not from God. So where did it come from? The enemy has done this. Matthew 13:28 (NLT) reads: "'An enemy has done this!' the farmer exclaimed. 'Should we pull out the weeds?' they asked."

From the above passage, you can see that the weeds of fear, abuse, emotional wounds, and trauma are planted by the enemy, whose only mission in your life is to kill, steal, and destroy. We live in a fallen world. So, there are things that may have happened in your life that you had no control over. What do you do? Stay down like the lame man who sat at the healing pool for thirty-eight years and when Jesus asked him if he wanted to be healed, instead of saying yes, decided to play pity party? John 5:7 (NLT) reads: "I can't, sir," the sick man said, "for I have no one to put me into the pool when the water bubbles up. Someone else always gets there ahead of me." Or would you rather take control of your healing and choose to be whole for yourself? The choice is yours.

The good news is, if you choose to be whole, this book will help you find the answers you need to make the choice to take up your bed and walk home, no longer bound by the pain and trauma from your past.

Like Julia, you may have been hurt, maimed, or harmed emotionally in the past, and you may have lost your identity because you are broken internally, but I want you to understand you have the power to choose your healing.

The inner work of transformation begins when you say yes to growth, change, and healing, going one step at a time until you come out of it, no matter how long it takes, and commit to the journey of healing.

How did Julia's past affect her as an adult? When it was time to choose a spouse, she settled for a man who was a narcissist. She didn't know this at that time because he camouflaged himself as a sweet, nice man, but looking back on it later, she realized the red flags were there, but she missed them because she didn't know what red flags in a relationship are and how to identify them. (We will look at red flags and how to identify them in the later chapters of this book).

After the honeymoon phase came the real deal for Julia. The honeymoon phase is the phase in a relationship or marriage where both of you still see eye to eye on all issues with little or no conflict because you're both enthralled by one another at that phase. I call this the fantasy island. After the first few weeks of marriage, reality hit Julia. Then she realized how mean and unkind her husband was. She found that this man only married her for what he could get out of her. These signs were present from the beginning—in the way he treated others, the way he spoke to people lower than him, etc. The signs may all be there, but if you are not yet whole in your mind, it will be hard to notice them. That is why you must be intentional about your healing. You cannot afford not to heal because the cost of refusing your healing is higher than the cost of healing.

EFFECTS OF ABUSE, TRAUMA, AND EMOTIONAL WOUNDS

The effects of abuse, trauma and emotional wounds cannot be overemphasized in our world today, and the telltale signs are everywhere. Let's look at a few of them:

- **People-pleasing and lack of boundaries.** Everyone knows someone who has an excessive need to please others, and many of us suffer from this problem ourselves. People who think they are nothing without validation from others will let others violate their personal boundaries just to please them.
- **Rebellion.** This has become a pandemic. Rebellious people refuse to obey authorities and defy set rules because of their past experiences.

- **Attention-seeking syndrome.** People who were deprived of love in their childhood will grow up seeking attention from others in order to fill their love tank.
- **Lack of self-governance/self-control.** Day by day, people are losing the ability to regulate their emotions and feelings. They behave however they like, wherever they are.
- **A deep lack of self-worth.** This often leads to accepting situations and circumstances that bring you shame and regret.
- **Addictions.** Substance abuse and other addictions are often an attempt to fill the void caused by pain or loss.
- **Suicide.** Sadly, some people take their own lives to supposedly end their suffering. There has been an alarming increase in the number of suicides in the world today.

The list goes on and on. I am spending this much time using different real events and stories to help you identify and understand what abuse, trauma, and emotional wounds are.

In the next chapter, we will be looking at how to heal from abuse, trauma, and emotional wounds because it is God's desire for you to live a meaningful and fulfilling life here on planet Earth.

Luke 12:32 (NLT) says, "So don't be afraid, little flock. For it gives your Father great happiness to give you the Kingdom." Now, you may ask, "What kingdom does God want to give me?" You will find the answer in Romans 14:17 (NLT): "For the Kingdom of God is not a matter of what we eat or drink, but of living a life of goodness and peace and joy in the Holy Spirit."

The Kingdom of God is actually a life filled with goodness, peace, and joy. Sadly, many daughters of the King of Kings are not experiencing this life that Jesus purchased for them on the Cross. Why? Because they are not living in the fullness of God's purpose for them. Many things can keep us away from enjoying this kingdom of God. For you, it may not be rape. It may be a different form of abuse, such as verbal, emotional, or mental abuse. Whatever type of abuse you may have endured, you must check inward and see if you have truly healed. I understand that it may be hard to process your healing alone. So please seek help from a professional therapist, a trusted friend, or a trained counselor who can walk you through the healing process with the help of the Holy Spirit. This may take weeks, months, or even years. It doesn't matter how long it takes. What is most important is that you heal completely before you step into the union called marriage.

Reflection

Get a notebook to write in and think back on how your past has affected your current situation. Identify patterns in your life, both good and bad. Then write down what you need to do to help you treat those negative patterns that arise because of traumas and abuse. I also want you to identify the key people who can work with you to help you heal and become the full version of yourself. As we journey together in this book, I pray that you will find the answers you so desperately need to help you enjoy this kingdom God has promised you.

CHAPTER 2

Woman, Thou Art Healed

I received a call one sunny afternoon. Eden, the lady on the phone, said to me, "I honestly don't think it's possible for me to forgive these men who used me. I did so much for them, and they had sex with me and then turned around and moved on with other women. I see their posts on social media, and they are using beautiful words to describe these women and their relationships with them. When I was with them, I did all I could to earn their love. I outdid myself and sacrificed so much for them, but they were not as loving or caring to me as they are to their current girlfriends. This hurts me more than I care to admit." She cried as she spoke. She was literally stalking these men's social media and placing her life on hold. She found it hard to forgive them for the hurt they inflicted on her and couldn't believe that they could be happy after what they had done to her. Oh, she definitely wanted them to get punished for their wickedness, which was a normal reaction.

It was a difficult conversation, to say the least. She couldn't believe that a man who hurt her terribly would end up marrying a virgin and living a beautiful life after all the evil he had done to her. How was this even fair? How was he able to get away with it? Was she expected to move on just like that? He stole her virginity and made her live in fear for many years, and still, he's the one who gets to be happy? How is this even fair?

Does this sound familiar? Sometimes things don't seem fair, and we honestly cannot explain why some things happen, but we must reach a place where we become willing to take charge of the things we can control.

Your wound or pain may not even be the result of a romantic relationship. It might be from your home or family members. It could be from a trusted friend. These hurts can come from different people whom we love and cherish or even respect, but whatever the case may be, there is hope for healing and total restoration for you.

How can you heal after experiencing trauma that you had no control over? How can you forgive yourself after making decisions you now regret or wish hadn't happened?

The answer is in truly coming to the Lord and allowing Him to deal with that wound. Your answer is in surrendering to Jesus and giving him the permission to heal you.

I told Eden she had to first forgive herself for her own mistakes. The first step to your healing is forgiving yourself. All it takes really is to say these words out loud: "[Your name], I forgive you for _____." Fill in the blank with whatever you need to forgive yourself for. "I forgive you for aborting that baby." . . . "I forgive you for treating yourself as less than you're worth." At the time, you didn't know any better.

Then I asked Eden to write the names of the men she was bitter against, call their names out loud, and say, "I forgive you." You see, the Earth operates by laws and principles. Just like the law of gravity, whatever goes up must come down. Of that you can be assured. There is also the law of sowing and reaping—each person will reap whatever they sow, good or evil, and it's not your place to take vengeance. It'll take its course. Your job is to focus on yourself and find ways to heal, and your healing starts with forgiveness—forgiveness of self and others.

As Eden made each of these statements of forgiveness, she wept deeply. These tears were pent-up emotions that had tied her down. She sobbed so much that it broke my heart. Forgiving those who wronged you is the hardest part, and that's okay. Forgiveness is not easy, but it is necessary if you truly want to be whole. It took hours for Eden to get these statements out, but it was a defining moment and part of her healing journey.

Now, I understand the journey to healing from trauma and emotional wounds is different from person to person. I still want you to know it is possible and it's God's desire for you to be healed and fully restored.

Just as I said to Eden, I also want to let you know that as you proceed on your healing journey, bitterness will periodically rise within you for yourself or the people who hurt you. That's natural. Whenever you feel this bitterness rising, repeat the process of letting go and ask the Holy Spirit to heal your heart and remove the pain. If you remain consistent and intentional, a time will come when the pain will be only a distant memory because the Holy Spirit will have taken it away completely.

There is power in total surrender. Let go and let God. Trust that he is capable and will heal your broken heart. I encourage you to find a Christian therapist or trained counselor who can help you navigate this journey. Most importantly, invite the Holy Spirit to heal the deep recesses of your wounded or traumatized soul.

INTERNAL THERMOSTATS

Internal thermostat means our ability to self-regulate our emotions. Many of us grew up in homes that did not teach us how to navigate emotional intelligence, so we do not know how to handle the different emotions we experience as humans. When you talk about internal thermostats, it involves three things:

- Identity
- Intention
- Association

Let us look at those three things one by one.

IDENTITY

Who are you? Your answer to this question defines you. Your answer to this question is the reason for your choices and decisions up to this moment in your life. Who are you? Your genuine answer will define who you decide to spend the rest of your life with. Who you are will determine the company you keep, the places you go, the food you eat, the clothes you put on, and the kinds of things you consume. Who you are shapes you through and through. So, this question of identity is one that you must keep in mind as you navigate through life and choose the path of healing.

What is your "why"? Your "why" is your strongest motivator, your greatest calling, and your guide through life.

Please pause and ask yourself those two questions: Who am I? What is my "why"? Answer these questions intentionally in a journal.

Now, whatever answers you may have written down, consider whether they align with the answer in 1 Peter 2:9 (NLT): "But you are not like that, for you are a chosen people. You are royal priests, a holy nation, God's very own possession. As a result, you can show others the goodness of God, for he called you out of the darkness into his wonderful light." This verse beautifully describes who God intended you to be. Are you this person of 1 Peter 2:9? No one can answer this question more accurately than you.

Since the fall of man in the Garden of Eden, man has defined himself based on the things he possesses or can acquire. But from the above passage, we see who you are:

1. A chosen person
2. A royal priest
3. A holy nation
4. God's very own possession

Your identity is in this verse. And, yes, it was tailor-made for you by the Grand Designer of all Humankind—God. I encourage you to commit 1 Peter 2:9 (NLT) to memory.

Often, when a lady has experienced abuse, trauma and emotional wounds, her identity is damaged and broken. And this is because the devil, your enemy, is a thief.

In John 10:10 (NLT), Jesus says, "The thief's purpose is to steal and kill and destroy. My purpose is to give them a rich and satisfying life." Through people, things, and events, the devil comes to steal your identity, kill your joy, and destroy your life's purpose. But God is a God of Restoration. He has come to restore you, to give you a rich life.

You may ask, "If God is so powerful and can do anything, why did He allow these bad things to happen to me? Where was God when this or that happened?" You see, my friend, God grieves over the wickedness of humanity, and He has already made a plan of escape and restoration for you through His son Jesus Christ. Does this mean every single person in the world will believe this and accept it? Unfortunately, the answer is no, even though that is His ultimate plan.

Luke 12:32 (NLT) says, "So don't be afraid, little flock. For it gives your Father great happiness to give you the Kingdom." The Father wants you to experience His Kingdom (love, peace and joy). Perhaps you can take a moment now to invite Him into your heart. He wants to help you heal and come out of every form of abuse, addiction, or other unhealthy lifestyle. He wants to help you live a life of purpose, a life that is rich and filled with a strong identity.

The word *healing* simply means the process of making something sound or healthy again. In this instance, it means restoring your identity to what it originally was supposed to be. That requires accepting that who you are is not based on the family you came from, your past experiences, or the things you possess, but rather that your identity is based on who God says you are. But your identity must be healed to be the person God says you are. This is not the time to play the victim or the blame game.

To be the true you, you must first find your identity in who you are in Christ: God's beloved child. Only when you do this can you be fulfilled and carry out His plans for you. When you, dear lady in waiting, submit to God, Christ will work in you and through you by His Spirit. In this way, you will be enabled to fulfill all the purposes He has for you—but you will do so in His strength, not your own. "What we have received is not the spirit of the world, but the Spirit who is from God, so that we may understand what God has freely given us" (1 Corinthians 2:12 NIV).

INTENTION

You must learn to reflect and introspect. This helps you question your motives and discover why you do the things you do. My life became richer and more meaningful the moment I began to reflect and introspect at the end of each day. Whenever I realize I haven't spoken or acted appropriately during my day, I make amends immediately if I can, or the same day, or the next day. This has brought so much positive change in my life.

Let me share an incredible story that exemplifies the power of reflection and introspection. Morris Cerullo, a world-renowned evangelist, once shared the profound story of how he met Jesus. He was born to an Orthodox Jew mom and an Italian dad, and his mom died when he was only two years old. He moved from one foster home to the other, ran away from home several times, and was always caught by the police. At age fourteen, he was already a defiant teenager.

One day, a nurse who attended a Baptist church was reflecting on her life. She went to the Lord in prayer, saying, "Lord, I have worked at this hospital for two years, and not once have I had the opportunity to share Your word with anyone or share the goodness of Jesus to a single soul." Then she looked out the window and saw young Morris Cerullo walking down the street. She had a witness in her heart to go show him the love of God. She reached out to him and started pouring love on him. She began by giving him some fruit and just simply caring. He resisted at first because he had never been shown real love and thought it was a farce. Well, she persisted until he came to her one day, and she drew him in with love. Then she finally got a chance to share the gospel of Jesus Christ with him. Morris Cerullo went on to publish over eighty books in his lifetime, traveled the world, and brought the message of salvation to over 130 nations in his over seventy years of ministry.

But how did it all begin? A Christian nurse reflected on her life's journey, and it led to a decision that has changed countless lives forever.

Can you imagine what you are missing when you do not spend time in reflection and introspection?

The Bible also teaches us on reflection and introspection in Luke 15:17–18 (NLT):

"When he finally came to his senses, he said to himself, 'At home even the hired servants have food enough to spare, and here I am dying of hunger! I will go home to my father and say, "Father, I have sinned against both heaven and you [. . .].'"

In reflection and introspection, you will find answers, make necessary changes, and alter the negative cycles in your life to more positive outcomes. When you deliberately begin to make the right choices to heal and regulate your emotions, you begin to love yourself more because you make better choices. You also start to live a more fulfilled life.

ASSOCIATION

Who is in your corner?

You are a reflection of the five people closest to you. With these people in mind, when you talk about healing, you must deliberately disassociate yourself from anything and anyone that is not helping you to heal from the wounds, abuse, and trauma of the past.

IN SUM: IDENTITY, INTENTION, ASSOCIATION

Do you see the sequence? First you need to know your identity. Then you can work on your intention, and finally you can address your associations.

Now, let's get back to our internal thermostats. How do you self-regulate? When you are hurt, sad, or frustrated, how do you manage your emotions? One thing that works for me is journalling. Journalling allows you to pour out your emotions, every bit of them, on paper. Another way to self-regulate is to speak to someone you trust, someone who can walk you through that experience. Or you might walk in nature to calm your mind and give yourself time to think. Find a method that works for you. The most important thing is to let out that emotion and not hold it in. Yes, you can apologize to yourself. Yes, you can tell yourself, "It's okay that I feel this way," but you must not stay that way. You must now move on. Pray and ask God for grace to walk in faith, but do not sink into any negative emotion. Do not let it drown you or open the door to the enemy, giving him a foothold.

$\mathcal{R}$eflection

Look inward and ask yourself these questions:

- Have I honestly addressed the hurt on my inside?
- Am I truly healed from the abuse?
- Do I think I am in a better place emotionally?
- Do I feel like I still carry emotional baggage around?
- Have I learned to self-regulate my emotions?

These are important questions you must ask yourself as a lady in the waiting room. Your happiness is solely your decision and your choice. Not even God can force you to be happy if you choose not to be. Nobody will make you happy if you choose to dwell on what is not working. Nobody will come and save you. You have to choose to rise and take responsibility for your healing and growth to enjoy the life that was created for you even before you were born. Do not continue to feel like a victim or play the victim card. Instead, learn to thrive and enjoy this gift called life.

CHAPTER 3
Identifying an Evil Foundation

While growing up as a pastor's kid, I noticed certain negative patterns in my family background—certain evil foundations—that, if not addressed, would cause me to make the wrong marital decision. I noticed that some of the women in my father's house and in my mother's family had terrible experiences before marriage and even in marriage.

I wrote down my observations and started to pray about them. In my prayers, I kept declaring that these things would not be my experience. I wrote down scriptures of God's promises about marriage, my husband, my future home, etc. For instance, I remember one time I was waiting on the Lord specifically concerning my education because I noticed that a lot of the women from my father's house did not go past a certain level in their education. People may call what happened next a coincidence, but I don't believe in coincidence. While waiting on the Lord, I had a vision in which some missionaries came to my village to preach the Gospel and spread education. However, my father's family opposed them. Just as Jesus commanded His disciples to shake the dust off their feet when leaving a city that rejected them, these missionaries shook the dust off against my father's family.

That action from my family members opened the door to such limitation, and the Lord instructed me on the next steps. At the time, I was the zonal vice president of NIFES (Nigeria Fellowship of Evangelical Students), an interdenominational fellowship for Christian students in university. After I had this revelation, NIFES had a national conference, and some missionaries joined the students at the event. I took my seed, prayed over it, and approached one of the foreign missionaries. I explained what the Lord had instructed me, and he called his wife over. Together, they prayed for me and released my family from the limitations. He took the seed from me, told me it belonged to the Lord, and then placed it into the offering box.

Afterwards, I was able to advance my education without any interference. Prior to this, I had a family member who had attempted to advance his education but was asked to leave the examination hall halfway through an exam. I didn't give this much thought because I felt it was just a mistake or pure coincidence, but now I understand it was not a coincidence. When the Lord opened my eyes to what had truly inspired this event, I knew something had to be done about it.

I believe Christ finished His work on the Cross and by sowing into the lives of the missionary, I was just walking into the fullness of the finished work of Redemption at the Cross. Even though Christ has redeemed us, we must do the walk to claim our redemption. Many people spend time arguing about whether or not these things are real and whether anyone needs to do anything about things like this. I know not to make a doctrine out of personal revelations; however, I also know repentance breaks yokes.

I am sharing this personal experience with you because I want to be transparent and emphasize the importance of standing on God's promises if you want to address negative patterns in your life. Standing on God's promises means believing them, confessing them and taking action. Even if you grew up in the church—even if, like me, you come from a pastor's family—you can't make positive changes in your life just by praying for what you want; your prayers must stand on God's promises.

Let me give you an instance from the Bible. The second book of Samuel 3:28–30 (AMPC) reads:

> When David heard of it, he said, I and my kingdom are guiltless before the Lord forever of the blood of Abner son of Ner. Let it fall on the head of Joab and on all his father's house; and let the house of Joab never be without one who has a discharge or is a leper or walks with a crutch or is a distaff holder [unfit for war] or who falls by the sword or lacks food! So Joab and Abishai his

brother slew Abner because he had slain their brother Asahel at Gibeon in the battle.

Joab killed an innocent man in a time of peace, and when King David heard of this, he cursed Joab and his father's house. This meant that everyone from Joab's family, including future generations not yet born, would experience the curses in verse 29 unless someone stood in to break that curse.

Those who did not understand this mystery may have wondered, "But, Joab, our ancestor was the commander of the army of Israel. Why are his family members experiencing this?"

This is why you must ask questions about your family and family patterns. Don't say it doesn't matter, because it does. And I truly believe in being intentional about whatever you do. Carl Jung said, "Until you make the unconscious conscious, it will rule your life and you will call it fate."

Now is the time to make these "happenstances" conscious so that they do not rule (and ruin) your life.

Reflection

Look at the family you come from. What patterns have you identified as common or unique to you and your family members? For some people, it is late marriage, for others, it is barrenness, certain illnesses, sudden death, no male children, broken homes, etc. What experiences are common to the women and men in your family that you do not want to repeat? Write these evil foundations down and take your list to God in prayers so that you can deal with then decisively once and for all. Then continuously speak in faith until your physical reality aligns with what God has said concerning you. Please do not leave anything to chance. Your Destiny is too precious to leave to chance.

Here are some prayers on identifying evil foundations:

1. By the power in the blood of Jesus, I disconnect myself from foundational powers that limit me, in Jesus' name. (Read Isaiah 54:17.)
2. I break the chain of heritage of fruitlessness, demonic limitation, untimely death, delay in marriage, delay in promotion, in the mighty name of Jesus. (Read Numbers 23:23.)
3. I reject the heritage of failure and poverty, rising and crashing, almost there but not there, retrogression, stagnation, and redundancy, in the mighty name of Jesus. (Read Psalms 91:10–12).

CHAPTER 4
The Battle of a Faulty Foundation

The devil is not all-powerful or all-knowing, but it may seem so because no one in your family has risen to challenge him and his works. If someone in a family rises and says, "Enough is enough," and stands on God's word and lives an intentional life, you will find that no faulty foundation can win in your life. Every family has its own unique battle, and someone in that family must rise up to say "No more" to that battle. Someone must decide that this battle ends in their time so that generations after them will experience victory. You can be that person in your family who will end the battle.

My mentor shared a story with me of five sisters who were not married. The oldest was fifty-six years old, and the youngest was thirty. They were all successful in their careers, but none of their relationships had ever led to marriage. They even sponsored some men they dated to either start a business or further their education, but somehow these men abandoned them for other ladies after they achieved financial independence or completed their education. At first the sisters thought this was a coincidence until they realized their cousins from their dad's side of the family were experiencing the same issue of successful careers but no life partners.

One of these ladies shared their struggles with my mentor, who took time to pray about this situation. In the place of prayer, the Lord showed her the battle of that foundation and instructed her on how to navigate this challenge. So, she asked the sisters and their cousins to take time off work and travel to their hometown for family prayers.

That night, as they rested from their journey, the Lord opened the eyes of my mentor by means of a dream. In that dream, my mentor saw a woman walking out of the family home, weeping and cursing her brothers until she wandered away.

After this revelation, when it was time for prayers, she asked the ladies if their dads had a sister, to which they replied in the affirmative. She asked, "So where is she?" They informed her that this sister now lived in another village. She had moved out before these sisters and cousins were even born, and none of them knew the full story because their dads had never talked about their sister. They had no information about what had transpired, but their deliverance was tied to this knowledge. Hosea 4:6 (AMPC) reads, "My people are destroyed for lack of knowledge."

So, they asked questions and found their way to the next village, where their aunt lived. My mentor had instructed them to plead with their aunt to forgive their fathers—her brothers—for whatever they had done to her.

She recognized her nieces the minute she saw them and wept like a baby upon seeing them. Apparently, their aunt had been in love with a man, and they were even planning to get married, but her brothers resisted the marriage because the man was poor. She was from a wealthy and influential family, and her brothers didn't think the man could take care of her. This man moved on and eventually married someone else. In pain, their aunt moved out of her father's house, but not before laying curses on her brothers. She told her brothers, "If what you have done to me is right, then let your daughters find love and get married and have their own homes, but if your actions to me were not right, then none of your daughters will find love or happiness, because you have robbed me of having joy with the man I love." After moving to this new village, she kept in contact with her lover and even had a child for him even though he was already married to someone else.

The lover's first wife had since passed away, and the aunt still wanted to marry her lover, so she asked her nieces to pray for them. That same day, they all traveled to this man's village, spoke to him, and found that he was still interested in marrying her. They organized a wedding that was held that same day. In the midst of celebration, music and laughter, their aunt stood up and proclaimed, "Just like I am getting married to the love of my life and there is joy and laughter and celebration, this is how my nieces will get married, and there'll be joy and continuous celebration for you."

So even though the nieces had traveled to the village to pray and deal with whatever was stopping their marriages, it definitely turned out in ways they couldn't have imagined. They returned to their various homes, and, in no distant time, each of them was happily married.

It is not uncommon to find revelations like this. In the Bible, during the reign of King David, there was famine in the land, and when David inquired of the Lord, he was told there was a breach of the covenant between Israel and the Gibeonites. Joshua and the elders had entered into a covenant with the Gibeonites not to kill them but to have them live among them as their servants, but Saul, in his zeal, killed them. The land of Israel suffered famine for three years because King Saul breached the covenant.

You will find this story in the book of 2 Samuel 21:1–9 (AMPC):

> There was a three-year famine in the days of David, year after year; and David inquired of the Lord. The Lord replied, It is on account of Saul and his bloody house, for he put to death the Gibeonites. So the king called the Gibeonites—now the Gibeonites were not Israelites but of the remnant of the Amorites. The Israelites had sworn to spare them, but Saul in his zeal for the people of Israel and Judah had sought to slay the Gibeonites—So David said to the Gibeonites, What shall I do for you? How can I make atonement that you may bless the Lord's inheritance? The Gibeonites said to him, We will accept no silver or gold of Saul or of his house; neither for us shall you kill any man in Israel. David said, I will do for you what you say. They said to the king, The man who consumed us and planned to prevent us from remaining in any territory of Israel, Let seven men of his sons be delivered to us and we will hang them up before the Lord at Gibeah of Saul, [on the mountain] of the Lord. And the king said, I will give them. But

the king spared Mephibosheth son of Jonathan, the son of Saul, because of the Lord's oath that was between David and Jonathan son of Saul. But the king took the two sons of Rizpah daughter of Aiah, whom she bore to Saul, Armoni and Mephibosheth, and the five sons of [Merab] daughter of Saul, whom she bore to Adriel son of Barzillai the Meholathite. He delivered them into the hands of the Gibeonites, and they hung them up on the hill before the Lord, and all seven perished together. They were put to death in the first days of barley harvest.

There are many kinds of faulty foundations that can limit you. A lot of families practice paganism, witchcraft and sorcery, for example. But the power in the blood of Jesus and His finished work at Calvary can cancel out all wickedness and overturn the evil.

There are foundations that eat heads and drink blood before they are destroyed. The question is whose blood and whose head? This is why you must make inquiries about the home you want to get married into, so that your blood or the blood of your children will not be used to settle any score before the foundation is destroyed.

Reflection

The point is that we all have foundations as long as we come from a family—no one fell from the sky—and each family has a unique issue they are dealing with. So I encourage you to look into your family and identify your unique battle—or ask your parents, family members, neighbors, etc. if you have no idea what your family's battle might be. Then engage in prayers and stand on God's promises for revelation on overcoming. Listen and obey whatever instruction the Lord gives you. Remember, we are fighting from a place of victory. And, by *fighting*, I mean we are engaging the Word of God by declaring the Word, renouncing the limitations and covenants, and placing a demand on the finished work of Jesus on the Cross. You want a marriage that is based on the right foundation. When you engage in this battle as an unmarried lady, you may deal with and resolve a lot of limitations and delays, including:

- First daughters not getting married or marrying late.
- The ladies having a child out of wedlock before marriage.
- Early widowhood.
- Women being the breadwinners of the home while the men lie back.
- Family involvement in witchcraft.
- The absence of male children.

Before getting married, I too identified the anomalies in my family, and I prayed against their occurrence in my life and in my home. In fact, when I met the man who became my husband, I asked lots of questions about his family. Some of them he was able to answer. For the ones he had no answers to, he asked his parents, and then, armed with the knowledge, we started addressing in prayers the issues we identified during our courtship. This gave us a solid foundation and an awareness that helped us become highly intentional in our choices in our marriage.

If you are already married and are facing problems in your marriage, look for the faulty foundation and pray accordingly. If you have children or other family members or loved ones who are married or separated and are facing similar battles, please do not hesitate to share this book with them, or send the following prayers to them and encourage them to pray.

Below are some powerful prayers you can pray against faulty foundations:

1. Lord, I repent of every willful error and demonic practice that has made me a lawful captive to demons and powers of darkness. Have mercy upon me in Jesus' name. Amen. (2 Chronicles 7:14)
2. By the covenant of the blood of Jesus, I command to expire and I destroy completely all the effects of strange covenants that have made me a lawful captive. (Isaiah 49:24–26)
3. I break every covenant and sacred oath that binds me to any strange altar by the covenant of the blood of Jesus, in Jesus' name. Amen. (Isaiah 8:9–10)
4. I walk out of every demonic prison door that my forefathers entered into in the mighty name of Jesus. (Isaiah 8:11–14)

CHAPTER 5
Dealing with a Faulty Foundation

A faulty foundation can limit and destroy a man and, if not addressed, can make a man question the faithfulness of God when in fact it's not God afflicting him. I recall after a session of my Ladies in Waiting Masterclass, a lady sent me a voice message. She was crying profusely and saying that the current module of the course must have been inspired by the Holy Spirit. She had never heard of such a thing as a faulty foundation before the session, even though she was a medical doctor and was well-traveled. She acknowledged there were lots of things in the module that resonated with her, because she could find traces of familial patterns that she thought were abnormal and needed to be addressed appropriately before marriage.

Believe me when I say that there are a lot of people like this who didn't know about faulty foundations. If you are one of them, congratulations, because your breakthrough is near. Start by conducting research about your family. Ask your parents, aunties, and other relatives about their families, childhoods, parents, marriages, etc.—anything that connects you to them. You might begin to discover family secrets and patterns no one has previously been willing to speak about.

A colleague mentioned to me that at her mother's funeral, she asked her younger brother questions about his current lifestyle and why he had changed his sex. He confided in her that when he was a child, their stepdad had molested him sexually multiple times, and that was the beginning of his losing his identity. She realized the same stepdad had molested her and their other siblings sexually. So, he was intimate with their mom and also with her children at the same time—such a level of depravity and corruption, and for more than forty years, it was a well-kept secret. Only after their mother's passing did all these secrets begin to be uncovered.

What family secrets do you need to begin to uncover so that you can begin to navigate emotional and spiritual healing and deliverance?

For you, dear lady who is about to get married, what family secrets does your husband-to-be know that you both need to begin to tackle in the place of prayers? If you ask and discover information that is deeper or greater than you can handle, now is a good time to walk away. A broken engagement is better than a broken marriage.

Marriage means entering your husband's family, and the truth is that the battle is from cradle to grave. If the foundation of his family is faulty, the opposition will become too much, especially if your husband is not on the same spiritual wavelength as you so that you can fight together.

Before I got married, I asked my parents and aunties questions, and the more I listened to sermons on these and prayed, the more revelations I received from the Lord concerning my family. I recall asking why nobody was talking about these things I discovered.

If this is your story, I hope you will find the stories, scriptures, and prayers in this book helpful in claiming your deliverance. It's important to approach the issue of a faulty foundation from a place of victory and a decision to prayerfully disengage and renounce the powers associated with the family limitations.

For instance, for some time, I would see snakes in my dreams and all kinds of weird encounters that I couldn't explain. I knew this wasn't normal, and I had to deal with it and renounce any existing covenant. So, I researched and learned that my village's name means community or gathering of snakes. I asked my dad about this, and he told me some stories surrounding the name. I also asked my aunt, who shared stories she had heard and seen growing up. Then I took this knowledge to God in prayers for victory. At the end, God liberated me, and all those weird encounters stopped.

So, ask questions about your family. What is happening to your siblings? What happened in your parents' marriage? Do not be laid back and expect things to change when you do nothing about it. Remember to check yourself, too. What is happening to you?

After you have gathered your answers and made your discovery, take it to God in prayer. The Holy Spirit will provide you with precise guidance on how to deal with each situation. Spiritual warfare is on a case-by-case basis; there is no one-size-fits-all approach. But one prayer theme that applies to everyone is this: Prayerfully ask the Lord to strip off you the inner lining that identifies you with your foundation. The inner lining of a man is the substance his soul is made of. This explains why certain people are predisposed to certain common traits or character flaws. The earth recognizes this inner lining, and that is why you must disassociate yourself from it.

There are families that have sorcery and witchcraft in their bloodline, and some people's parents, grandparents, etc. were witch doctors or worshippers of the devil. When one comes from such a bloodline and gives one's life to Christ by becoming born again, one must continue in the Word by meditating on it intentionally and praying consistently. Otherwise, when push comes to shove, when faced with life's pressure, the person may be tempted to go back to their roots. They may find themselves imagining and releasing wicked thoughts against those who have offended them. This impulse will come naturally to them without struggle if they have not renewed their mind in God's word. You may not be from an occultic bloodline, but we all have the part of us that thinks such thoughts, especially when it seems that God's way isn't working as fast as we want it to. Renewing your mind is a *must* if you are to walk with the Lord in freedom and deliverance.

Reflection

Here is one important prayer to pray:

Holy Spirit, show me the deep secrets that I need to know in the battle of dealing with my foundation. (1 Corinthians 2:10)

After you have said this prayer, listen and obey the divine instructions that come with your answer. The Lord is interested in your deliverance. If you don't deal with a faulty foundation, it'll limit you from meeting the right person for you or from getting married at God's time for you, and it can also limit the quality of life you have in your marriage if you are already married. Remember that not all delays are from God, and you must tarry in the place of prayer to claim what is yours.

CHAPTER 6
Self-Discovery and Loving Yourself

I once met a man whom I thought I was going to marry. He was born again, and I liked him more than I liked the other suitors I had at the time. In fact, he was a preacher and my kind of man, or so I thought, until I started the journey of self-discovery and walking with God. I discovered that our core values did not align. The Lord specifically spoke to me about the life He wanted me to live, and I knew that if I married this wonderful man, I would be miserable because our values did not align. If I had proceeded with the marriage without this self-discovery, we would have had untold friction and heartaches in the future.

As an unmarried lady, your knowledge of who you are will inform your choice of a spouse. You must answer this crucial question before you even consider settling down with anyone. This journey to self-discovery starts when you work on improving yourself.

The moment a lady gets to her early twenties, her family and friends begin to expect that she'll bring a man, and if the lady does not follow this pattern, she becomes a prayer point for her parents and friends. By the time she gets to twenty-nine or thirty years old and is still unmarried, she becomes depressed and worried or even desperate because the mindset is that time is running out.

John Maxwell, in his book *The 15 Invaluable Laws of Growth*, writes, "Time has a way of getting away from most people, yet time is what life is made of. Everything we do requires time, yet many people take it for granted. How you spend your time is more important than how you spend your money. Money mistakes can be corrected. But once time has passed, it's gone forever."

My dear lady in waiting reading this book, now is the time for your personal development. Now is the right time to develop the right relationships. So, next, we will look at self-discovery in two parts: people/environment and personal growth.

PEOPLE/ENVIRONMENT

One way to gauge whether you're growing and in a conducive environment for growth is to ask yourself whether you're looking forward to what you're doing or constantly looking back at what you've done. If the future seems dull, routine, or confining, it may be time to consider making changes so that you can grow, spend time with great people, visit inspiring places, attend meaningful events, read impactful books, and listen to enriching content.

What do people need?

- The right soil to grow in. What nourishes us? *Growth.*
- The right air to breathe in. What keeps us alive? *Purpose.*
- The right climate to live in. What sustains us? *People.*

There is a famous saying that if you put a pumpkin in a jug when it's the size of a walnut, it will grow to the size and shape of the jug and never get bigger. This also applies to our thinking as humans. Don't allow that to happen to you.

As the Italian proverb says, "Keep company with good men, and you will increase their number." What kinds of "good" people should we spend our time with? People with integrity. Positive people. People who are ahead of us professionally. People who lift us up instead of knocking us down. People who take the high road, never the low. And, above all, people who are constantly growing.

You cannot make the growth journey alone—not if you want to reach your full potential. The most significant factor in anyone's environment is the people around them. If you change nothing else in your life but this, you will increase your chances of success tenfold. So, think long and hard about who you spend the most time with, because wherever they are headed, so are you.

So, instead of spending your unmarried years waiting for a man to come along or surfing through the internet or social media and feeling very unfortunate about your life, why not adjust your mindset and decide to take charge of what you can control and trust God with the things you cannot control? Psalm 34:22 (NKJV) says, "The Lord redeems the soul of His servants, And none of those who trust in Him shall be condemned." As you trust in Him, you shall not be desolate.

I meet many unmarried ladies who are so worried about being single, it's as if their entire lives are put on hold because they are waiting for a man. Some ladies even begin to self-sacrifice for a man who pretends to be interested in them, and when he walks away, they begin to contemplate suicide, as though life is over for them or their life and joy were dependent on him.

My dear lady in waiting, singlehood isn't a death sentence. Your happiness is not dependent on another person. You have the power to choose to be happy. Please don't self-sabotage because you haven't found the right man yet. Live your life, and trust God that all will align at the end of the day. Do not give another person the power to control your happiness. Happiness is a choice. And it's yours to make.

SELF-DOUBT VERSUS SELF-LOVE

We live in an era when self-care is preached in many circles. So, before I tell you about self-care, let's first talk about self-doubt and what it can do to you.

Many ladies do not love themselves because many of us were not taught how to, nor did we learn on our own. We would rather wait for Mr. Right to love us and fill our love tank. Jesus said in Matthew 22:39 to love your neighbor as you love your own self. This means you cannot give what you do not have. You must first learn to love yourself before you can love someone else. The love has to start from within, and your unmarried years are the best time to get to know and understand you.

This is the best time to court yourself—to love *you*. Now is the time to do for yourself everything you expect a man to do to you and for you. Treat yourself right first, because you will soon realize that in marriage you have to learn to love unconditionally, and it starts with loving yourself unconditionally.

When I was working on these things, there were two major points of focus that helped me deal with my self-doubt. The first was taking responsibility for everything that happened to me. True, you can't help it if your partner cheated on you or if you were bullied as a kid, but you can control the story you wrap around it. You can choose to see the bitter experience as a lesson and use the feedback from it to make better decisions in the future. Your partner cheated on you, but now you know what signs to look for in your next relationship. Somebody beat the crap out of you when you were a kid, but now you can use that fire to grow mentally and physically stronger. A work colleague did you a bad turn, but now you know the kind of person you can or can't trust going forward. All failures provide feedback if you choose to look for it.

The second point of focus that helped me deal with self-doubt was a story about Michelangelo, the Italian Renaissance sculptor, painter, architect, and poet. When Pope Julius II asked Michelangelo to paint the frescoes on the ceiling of the Sistine Chapel, Michelangelo hesitated. He questioned whether he was a good enough painter for such an important project. He was best known as a sculptor, not a painter. Also, fresco painting is challenging because it has to be completed while the plaster is still wet; there is no room for error. He finally agreed to do the frescoes, but he battled self-doubt throughout the process. He even wrote a sonnet lamenting the difficulty of the endeavor, part of which can be translated as "I am no painter." The great Michelangelo felt so challenged and deterred by self-doubt that he believed he was a terrible painter. Yet he managed to create a magical work of art that the whole world celebrates today. Every time I question my ability as a writer, speaker or coach, I remember Michelangelo's words, and they help me deal with my own self-doubt. It always serves me to know that one of the greatest painters of all time questioned his painting ability.

Reading that story for the first time made me realize that everyone has self-doubt, even the greats.

To get your ladder up against the right wall, you must first learn to ignore the voice in your head that's saying you can't do it. Understanding that self-doubt doesn't go away has made the biggest difference to me over the past several years. We all have self-doubt in different areas of life, but the key is to acknowledge the self-doubt, feel the fear, and do it anyway.

One of my tools to stay on course when self-doubt creeps in is the acronym WIN—What's Important Now. It may take years to master yourself and your inner thoughts, but when you focus on What's Important Now (WIN), even the biggest goals can be broken down into the smallest tasks. If you're trying to lose a hundred pounds, you must shift your focus from the end goal to losing the first pound, then the second pound, and then the third. If you want to run a marathon, don't focus on the end goal of 26.2 miles; rather, focus on running one mile, then two miles, and so on, until you achieve your goal. By doing a task step by step, we get ahead figuratively and literally. Once you apply the philosophy that nothing happens overnight and the struggle makes the victory even sweeter, then success becomes almost inevitable.

We have the ability to make conscious decisions to change our attitudes, our skill sets, and our lives. Again, it just comes down to learning to control negative self-talk and changing how we see things.

Here is another exercise that can be incredibly effective but may be uncomfortable to do: asking others what weaknesses they see in you. Speaking from personal experience, I can tell you this exercise isn't easy, but it can be very helpful in overcoming our blind spots—that is, the characteristics we fail to see in ourselves but that are so obvious to others. The key is to ask for feedback from people who truly want to see you improve. I do this exercise with the people in my inner circle regularly. Remember to ask for brutally honest answers.

In the beginning, the feedback you get can be difficult to take in. I remember the first time I asked for feedback; I was told that I was self-absorbed and too obsessed with success, and that I failed to prioritize the people closest to me. This feedback hurt a lot because it was true. But I am grateful for it, because it helped me realize that I did put myself above others when it came to making decisions, and that my drive was focused on the accumulation of things: cars, clothes, status, basically all the things I thought would make me feel superior to others.

I like to think of such conversations as one's first workout in the gym or the first time one does any new physical exercise. The first workout is always painful, leaving us sore for a few days. Afterwards, as we become more adapted to the training, we become stronger. Just like the gym makes us physically stronger, having difficult but meaningful conversations makes us mentally and emotionally stronger. Therefore, lean into the discomfort of uncomfortable conversations with the right people, and see how quickly your life begins to change for the better.

John Assaraf tweeted, "The comfort zone is a beautiful place, but nothing ever grows there."[1] I'll go one step further and add that the discomfort zone is a beautiful place because everything grows there!

Asking for criticism may seem counterintuitive to working on your self-doubt, but facing these insecurities makes you mentally tougher. When you own your weaknesses, wear them as badges of honor, and begin to improve on them, your self-confidence will skyrocket, eliminating all your self-doubt. Don't let your self-doubt determine your self-worth.

If getting your ladder up against the right wall is the first step in rewriting your mindset, and getting over your self-doubt and building confidence are the second and third steps, then the next obstacle you need to tackle is caring too much about what other people think about you. Learning to inoculate yourself from the opinions of others, especially those whose opinions don't really matter, can free you to do everything that makes you happy.

---

[1] John Assaraf (@johnassaraf), Twitter (now X), April 16, 2015, 9:31 pm UTC, https://x.com/johnassaraf/status/588816956263923712.

NO-COMPLAINING ZONE

I'm reaching out to everyone who is now living as I once did—complaining about life, feeling like a victim, and believing that life happens *to* them and not *for* them. If you're not happy with where you are, who you are, or what you have, remember this: You can move and change. You are not a tree! Instead of complaining, find a solution. Complaining about your situation is just a subtle way of playing the victim card. True, you are not repeating "Woe is me," the traditional mindset we associate with victims, but complaining is even more dangerous as it hides the truth of what you are really doing. It's the mask you wear when you want to be a victim but can't or don't want to admit it.

Tell me what you do every day, and I'll tell you where you'll be in a year, five years, or ten years. When I hear people constantly complaining about their situation—their job, their relationship, their health, their body or fitness level—I know 95% of them are going to be in the exact same place in five or ten years, complaining about something else or, worse, the same thing. Nothing changes until you start making new decisions. If this sounds like you, know that you can change—and I implore you to do so.

Who you've been up until now is not who you're becoming. If you're reading this book and you're what I call a "cloaked complainer"—your cloak or mask covers your victim mentality—you should make the conscious choice to join the 5% who decide to own it, control it, and change it.

And don't beat yourself up if this is how you've been up until now. I was one of the 95%, too. I was the queen of excuses, a cloaked complainer for years. So, you're in good company. But once I became aware of it, I made the decision to change.

The above discussion brings me to my next point: Should you ever complain? Does it have any benefits?

The truth is that you will probably be much better off if you stop complaining, but it doesn't just happen. I had to start small. I undertook a thirty-day no-complaining challenge to see how badly ingrained my tendency to complain was.

The challenge is exactly as it sounds—no complaining for thirty days. I told all my closest friends I was doing it and gave them permission to call me out if I faltered. Also, if I found myself complaining, I would pause mid-sentence and say out loud, "No complaining for thirty days."

I'm not going to lie to you—seeing the challenge through was incredibly difficult! The first time I tried the challenge, I was already pretty good at owning everything I did, and I wouldn't have classified myself as "a complainer." Yet, when I started the challenge, I realized I had a few default complaints that I was unaware of: traffic and the weather. I didn't even realize I had been doing it until that point.

After three days, I set "no complaining zone" as my phone screensaver, which helped me considerably. As I was almost always with my phone, every time I unlocked the screen, it served as a subtle visual reminder of my task for the day.

At the end of thirty days, I had significantly reduced the frequency of my mini complaints. I was able to catch myself mid-sentence and rewire my mindset in nearly any situation. If I started to complain about the rain, I would catch myself and remind myself, "Yes, it's raining, but a blind man would love to see it all the same," or if I heard somebody else complain about the weather to me, I would reply, "The weather may be bad, but the day is awesome." It's worth noting that the first time you speak like that, most people won't know how to respond; they will just look at you blankly for a while, but they will adjust as you continue. It's fun to experiment with this challenge for the reactions alone!

You may read this and wonder how something as small as not complaining about the weather could impact your life in any way, shape, or form. My response: "Tell me how you do the small things, and I'll tell you how you'll handle the big things." I am confident that if you train yourself to stop complaining about little things like the weather, you'll soon notice that you stop complaining about the bigger things, too: your boss, your spouse, your colleagues, and so on. How you do anything is how you do everything.

Complaining is for victims. We usually associate victims with passivity—quiet, timid people who don't act. But the truth is, actively complaining is just as much, if not more, a victim mindset. It's dangerous because it doesn't fit the usual image of victimhood, making it harder to recognize in yourself. Don't be fooled!

Remember that how you handle the small things is how you will handle the big ones. Start with the thirty-day no-complaining challenge—or even a three-day or three-hour challenge—and take ownership of your life. You can't change what you don't own.

There is no perfect time to do anything. Now is the time. Do you want to go on a vacation? Do not wait until you're married to do so. Go ahead and do it now. Do you have unused china in your kitchen cabinet that you are preserving for future use? Now is the right time to use it. What about that lingerie that you have been keeping for when you get married? My dear single lady in waiting, find it, put it on, and look good for yourself. This is you learning to love you.

Learn a craft or a sport, read books—essentially, do something for you. Love you and appreciate you first. Women are sacrificial in nature; we give and give, sometimes without thinking of ourselves. While it is good to be sacrificial, it is equally good to be balanced.

After I met my husband and I knew he was the right person for me, we had a seven-year waiting period. While waiting, I would sometimes complain, asking when this period would be over. Thankfully, I had a friend who kept reminding me to maximize that season and make the most of it. Fast-forward to this day, I'm married with three toddlers, and I don't look back with regrets because I maxed out that season by learning to love me. This self-investment has helped me in my journey as a mom and wife. I assure you that pouring love on yourself will also help you in your journey as a mom and wife.

Reflection

Oftentimes, we see two types of women: a very selfish lady who thinks only about herself and a selfless lady who doesn't know how to care for herself because she gives and gives until she is spent. Your goal should be becoming a balanced woman who is not on the extreme of either group. Cultivating a relationship with yourself and discovering your identity in Christ, why you exist, will elevate your mind and properly position you for the excellent home you will nurture.

CHAPTER 7

Discovery and Walking in Purpose

As a teenager, I came across a quote that drastically revolutionized my life and altered how I made decisions and choices. This quote is attributed to Myles Munroe: "If the purpose of a thing is not known, abuse is inevitable."

God will bring you opportunities in the form of relationships and circumstances. If you do not know why you are on this earth, if you do not discover your unique identity and make decisions and choices according to your unique purpose, you will abuse these opportunities, make excuses, and blow up your chances of living an intentional and fulfilled life.

So, how do you discover your purpose as a lady?

First things first, you must understand that you are not a mistake, regardless of the circumstances of your birth. You were created by an intentional God who loves you and who has a grand design for your life. I know some people were born into families where their birth was anticipated and their parents looked forward to their birth. But for some others, their birth was not anticipated, or they were seen as a mistake. Whichever category you belong to doesn't take away the fact that you are created for a unique purpose.

The best way to experience fulfillment in your life is to find God's purpose and then work with Him to fulfill it. To truly live in purpose and fulfill your purpose, you must understand the purpose of God for humanity.

Romans 12:1 (AMPC) reads: "I appeal to you therefore, brethren, and beg of you in view of [all] the mercies of God, to make a decisive dedication of your bodies [presenting all your members and faculties] as a living sacrifice, holy (devoted, consecrated) and well pleasing to God, which is your reasonable (rational, intelligent) service and spiritual worship."

Let's look at this excerpt from Myles Munroe's book *Understanding the Purpose and Power of a Woman*:

> When Jesus came to earth, He showed us the mark that we are to hit. So whatever He says is what we're supposed to pursue. He showed us God's original plan so that we could have something to aim at. We should never accept what we currently have as the norm. Even though it may be the current trend, if it's not what God intended, it's abnormal. We should never live so below our privilege that we begin to believe a lie and call it truth. When you begin to understand and live in the purposes of God, people may become very uncomfortable with you. When you tell them, "Look, I know what it is to be a woman. I went to the Manufacturer and got the right Manual," they may say, "Oh, no, that's an old manual; it's out of date.

That sums up everything you need to understand about discovering your purpose. Discovering your purpose lies first in your relationship with the Lord. No, I am not talking about just going to church but having a personal walk with Him and leaning into the Holy Spirit in obedience. Truly knowing God and partnering with the Holy Spirit will help you discover your uniqueness. And when you do, you go all in, unapologetically.

I am the last of six children, and my parents said my birth was a mistake. You see, they already had three girls and two boys, so they were not looking for another child. They decided to abort the pregnancy since I was unwanted and unplanned. But God had other plans (I say this with a chuckle). My mom was on her way to the hospital for the abortion procedure when she decided to stop briefly at her friend's place. Now this friend asked my mom where she was going, and after much prodding, my mom confided in this friend about this unplanned pregnancy. My mom had valid reasons to terminate the pregnancy—she'd had her five babies by C-section, and her life was at risk if she went ahead to have me. As a mom myself who's had three C-sections, I can imagine my mom's fear at the time. Still, her friend encouraged her to keep the baby and trust God to help her through it.

My mom agreed not to abort me, and halfway through my pregnancy, her younger son (the fifth child) died. So, she hoped and prayed I'd be a boy child since she already had three girls. Alas, I came out as a girl. She was so disappointed that she refused to carry me much when I was a newborn. But as I grew and walked in the path that God had designed for me, my mom became grateful that she hadn't aborted me. The child that was a mistake later became a blessing.

Just like me, your story may be one of rejection or unpleasantness. I know how you feel, but you must not let it define who you are or who you will become. You must make the choice to stand out and step into your high calling in Christ. Leave the past in the past, and pursue what God has designed for you, just as Apostle Paul said in Philippians 3:13 (AMPC): "I do not consider, brethren, that I have captured and made it my own [yet]; but one thing I do [it is my one aspiration]: forgetting what lies behind and straining forward to what lies ahead."

While I was growing up, our next-door neighbors had a daughter about the same age as my older sister. As soon as she turned thirty, she became agitated and deeply worried about her age. She was concerned that she and my older sister were getting older and still not married. She would encourage my sister to find a solution quickly so that age wouldn't catch up with them. Next thing we heard was that she was getting married, and we were so happy for her. My sister visited her friend just before the wedding but felt that something wasn't right with the marriage. She couldn't place her finger on the real issue, but she noticed that her friend wasn't looking very happy. I prayed with my sister about this, and then she approached her friend to share her concerns. She advised her friend to pray about it and not to rush into such an important decision, but she couldn't force the friend to do anything the friend didn't want to do.

One year into the marriage, her friend separated from the man due to irreconcilable differences. She also had several health challenges from the stress of the marriage, and we lost her by the end of the second year. She was so eager to get married at age thirty because, according to her and society, her biological clock was ticking. By age thirty-two, she was gone. Could this death have been avoided? *Yes!*

You see, it's important we discover the reason we are born. Why are you on earth? Do you have a relationship with your Creator? Have you discovered the reason you are here? As an unmarried lady, are you actively seeking God and putting Him first in your decisions and choices, allowing His Spirit to direct your steps? Are you allowing God to lead you? If you allow the Lord to lead you, He will show you in time what His purpose is for you each season of your life and also lead the right man to you.

A woman can abuse her nature and purpose if she doesn't understand why she is the way she is. In addition, a woman who does not understand her purpose can be a detriment to a purposeful man in the same way that a man who doesn't understand the woman's purpose can be a detriment to the woman's purpose.

If you have noticed marital delay, I encourage you to seek the Lord and let Him reveal to you what the issue might be. Many people underestimate the limitations their family roots and foundations or curses have placed on them. This is not to overestimate the power of the devil—NO WAY—but we must acknowledge that evil forces exist and treat them accordingly. Please return to chapter three to deal with this foundation issue.

You also cannot talk about walking in purpose without talking about the relationships you keep—the people in your life. Remember that your life is a reflection of the people in your circle. As we pray, we should also invest our time, talent, and treasure in finding and maintaining meaningful relationships. Become personally involved in the lives of others. Spend significant time with those you'd like to reach, and then make sure your plan is represented on your calendar or in your day planner. Invite your friends out for lunch or dinner or to your home for coffee. Do things together. Attend plays, sporting events, art exhibits. Go shopping. Share special days—birthdays, graduations, holidays, weddings, births. Visit, call, or write to each other. Join a service club such as a book club or a library board. Take a class through your park district, or join an interest club (gardening, cooking, quilting). Volunteer in your local school or hospital or other charitable organization. Open your home to the neighborhood. Be the most hospitable home on the block to children and adults. There are so many ways to build quality relationships. I know from experience that some seasons of our lives are more conducive to evangelism than others. Find what works for you and be open to trying new things.

Reflection

After salvation, look around your church family or community for what you can do for the Lord, then talk to the Lord about it. Allow Him to lead you and show you what to do next, and once you receive His instructions, run with them. I tell you that you will reap the dividends of joy, fulfillment, and walking in your purpose. And of course, you will meet your spouse when you are in the will of God.

The Bible tells us about Ruth, who was walking in her purpose by serving her mother-in-law, Naomi. It may not have been the most convenient thing for her because her purpose took her away from her family and made her an immigrant in a foreign land, but in her service, she met Boaz, who later became her husband. Nobody can go wrong when walking in purpose.

I remember when I was serving in my local church as a single. With my natural eyes, no one from this local assembly could have qualified to be my husband. But guess what? When the time was right, I met my future husband at a work location. At the time, I didn't even know I would be married to him because entering a relationship wasn't on my mind. But God rewards those who walk in purpose.

Ask yourself . . . am I walking with the Lord? Have I left what I perceive to be my assignment due to pressure? If you have, now is a good time to make a U-turn. Spend time discovering yourself. Find out what you love and do not love. What do you find exciting or fulfilling? Your answers to these questions will lead you to discovering your purpose. Spend time getting to know you. Take charge of what you can control as you trust the Lord to bring the right man.

CHAPTER 8
Walking with God and Consecration

Walking with God is an ongoing, daily decision to choose God's ways over our own ways.

I read a story that demonstrates the discipline it takes to walk with God.

A mom ordered some items online, but the items were delayed for three months. She needed these items urgently and so went into the store with her daughter. While they were waiting for the clerk to return with yet another lame excuse, this mom fumed and thought to herself that she was going to give the clerk a piece of her mind. Holly, her daughter, gently placed her hand on her mom's arm, called her mom, and said, "Let's be different. Let's act like Christians." These words brought both happiness and shame to her mom. On one hand, she was happy that what she had been teaching her child for years had sunk in. On the other hand, she was ashamed because she had failed to do the very thing she taught her daughter. As Christians, we must do as God commands us when it favors us and when it doesn't.

Walking with God has to be an intentional daily action, and it becomes easier when we surround ourselves with a circle of people who walk with God. This serves as a check when we need to check ourselves.

Matthew references the garden prayer in Matthew 26:39 (NIV): "Going a little farther, he fell with his face to the ground and prayed, 'My Father, if it is possible, may this cup be taken from me. Yet not as I will, but as you will.'" This prayer reveals Jesus' intense desire to submit to God's will no matter what it cost Him. He shows us that the will of God is more important than life itself.

In our walk with God, we must renew our minds by creating time to fellowship with the Lord, for how can we claim to be in a relationship with one we do not spend time with? It's in spending time with Him in prayers and by studying the Word that our senses are sharpened to discern His voice and understand His will. Then we can deliberately make choices during our day to honor Him.

PRACTICAL WAYS OF WALKING WITH GOD

I encourage you to incorporate God into everything you do daily. One way to do this is through meditation. Psalm 1:2–3 (AMPC) says: "But his delight and desire are in the law of the Lord, and on His law (the precepts, the instructions, the teachings of God) he habitually meditates (ponders and studies) by day and by night. And he shall be like a tree firmly planted [and tended] by the streams of water, ready to bring forth its fruit in its season; its leaf also shall not fade or wither; and everything he does shall prosper [and come to maturity]."

So how do we meditate? The Bible says meditation should be continual, "day and night" (Psalm 1:2; Psalm 119:97; Psalm 119:148; Psalm 63:6). You can make meditation part of your devotions, your quiet time with God. But even your busy schedule can be punctuated with scriptural meditation—in the car, at lunch break, while waiting for a bus. Write a text on a card and slip it in your pocket or purse. Pull it out in a spare moment. Murmur it. Memorize it. Pray it. Say it. Share it.

When I speak with unmarried ladies who believe that time is leaving them behind, I always sense this deep worry about getting old and not finding a life partner yet. Worse is that society (family and friends) doesn't make it better for them. They are constantly facing pressures from different angles, even though some of it may be coming from a place of love. I understand this struggle, but I also want to remind you to rest in Him. Live in the awareness that God is your Father, He cares about you, and He has a plan for your marital destiny. He knows you want to settle down and build your own home. He knows that, and he is preparing you for that home.

Worrying doesn't help. It only leaves you feeling desperate, unhappy, or unfortunate, and these negative thoughts can begin to influence your choices and decisions, making you settle for less than God's best for you. Meditate on God's promises for you day and night. Memorize his promises so that when the thoughts of running late begin to surface, you can immediately begin to confess these promises and quiet the voice of doubt and fear. Say to yourself: God will not leave me or forsake me. He is my Father, and I will not lack my mate.

Whenever my mind begins to worry about an issue I have no control over, rather than playing scenarios in my mind, I find a scripture that relates to that situation and pray it. This helps me refocus my gaze on the Lord's promises about that issue.

How does meditating on God's promises bring the man? Simple. When you meditate on God's promises, instead of just thinking about the things that are not, you are calling them forth as though they were (Romans 4:17b). You see, my friend, life operates by certain principles. For instance, the law of gravity says anything that goes up must come down. It's a law that is enforced regardless of where you are on earth, your skin color, weight, height, or religion. It's the same with the principle of meditation. Some call it the law of attraction; it's the same thing.

CONSECRATION

"I am the Lord, and there is no other; apart from me there is no God" (Isaiah 45:5 NIV). There is no other God besides the Lord, yet He is a God of relationship, not isolation. He desires someone of His nature and likeness whom He can love. Therefore, God's primary motivation in the creation of man was love. He created man because He wanted to share His love with a being like Himself, a being created in His image. So, the word *consecration* is not the exclusive preserve of ministers or even pastors. Consecration simply means dedication. And in this regard, it simply means living a life dedicated to pleasing your Father, who wants to be in a relationship with you. So, whether it's in your choice of music, dressing, lifestyle, or anything else, the goal should be to please the Lord. Remember, you cannot give what you don't have.

God and humanity were made for one another. It doesn't matter whom else you love, you aren't ever going to be satisfied until you love God. No matter how many relationships you get into and how many gifts you buy for others, when it's all over, you will still be lonely. Why? Because the Person whom you were made to love above all else, God, doesn't have the place in your life that He needs to have. You were made to love God. Your love was designed to be fulfilled in Him.

When God said, "Let us make mankind in our image, in our likeness" (Genesis 1:26 NIV), He was saying, in effect, "Let us make someone to love, and call it 'man.' Since we want man to be the object of our love, we're going to make man in our own image and in our own likeness. This creation will be just like us." Therefore, when God made man, He essentially drew man out of Himself, so that the essence of man would be just like Him.

"God is spirit, and his worshipers must worship in the Spirit and in truth" (John 4:24 NIV). We worship God with our spirits, not with our gender. That means before God, whether you are a man or woman, your spirit does not depend upon your wife or husband.

Your ultimate love life is fulfilled when you first love God and walk with Him. This is the essence of consecration.

The Bible says that every person must stand on his own feet before God (Romans 14:10). God is going to deal with us Spirit to Spirit. Therefore, spiritually, God does not care whether you are male or female. Your relationship with God is not dependent on whether you are a male or a female. He is most concerned with your spirit man. You must come to God through your spirit. The presence of the spirit man within us is why the Bible says that all men have sinned, rather than that "men and women have sinned." Romans 5:12 (NKJV) reads, "Death spread to all men, because all sinned." The word *men* in this verse is translated from the Greek word *anthropos*, meaning human.

Some ladies want to marry a man who is more spiritual than she is, and this is fine, but I don't think that this should be your core goal. A better perspective would be for you to develop intimacy with your Father, and when you do this, He will give you the man who's just right for you, one of God's sons.

Here is the story of my friend, Rose. Rose, who was the first child of her parents, lost both parents at different times while she was still single. Faced with the task of caring for five younger siblings plus navigating her career as a recent graduate, she was concerned about getting married. She worried that no man would want to get married to her and take on the added responsibility of looking out for her siblings while trying to build their marriage. Thankfully, she knew to take her worry to God. After waiting on the Lord in prayers, she did her part by walking in active service for God while growing her career at the same time. Guess what? She met her husband in the place of service, and all the things she considered as her disadvantages didn't mean a thing to the man. He was happy to take on the responsibility of helping raise her younger siblings. In fact, he became the big brother they never had, and he accepted them genuinely.

$\mathcal{R}$eflection

Never underestimate the power of walking with God. Your seeming impossibilities or fears will fly out the window because, with God, nothing is impossible. And remember that he that must come to God must be pure, and that is where consecration comes in. Consecration is a currency for the power of God. Living a consecrated life as an unmarried lady simply means becoming deliberate in the music you listen to, the choice of company you keep, how you dress . . . everything you do.

So, you see, there can be no consecration if a relationship with God is not active. Otherwise, it will just be an outward show of religion to impress people. God is not moved by religion; He is moved by our desire to fellowship with Him. I challenge you to say to yourself: "I live for the audience of One, and that one is God."

Here are some scriptures to memorize and meditate on when worry fills your heart:

- "Not one shall lack her mate." (Isaiah 34:16 NKJV)
  Prayer: I shall not lack my mate in Jesus's name.
- "He who finds a wife finds what is good and receives favor from the Lord." (Proverbs 18:22 NKJV)
  Prayer: I find my spouse and my spouse finds me in Jesus's name.
- "Then the Lord God said, 'It is not good for the man to be alone. I will make a helper who is just right for him.'" (Genesis 2:18 NLT)
  Prayer: Thank you, Lord, that you have made me a helper fit for my husband, and that you are bringing us together in marriage without any delay, in Jesus' name, amen.

Start now to change your thinking, and watch as your life begins to go in the direction of your words. Whenever you find yourself worrying about your marital status, speak the Word of God back to those thoughts, and watch the shift that will happen in your life.

CHAPTER 9
Obedience and Service

Walking in obedience to God's will for your life is easier when you see God as your Father. The Bible says in Malachi 1:6, "If I am your Father, where is my honor?" I once attended a conference where our coach taught us that God, as our Father, wants the highest good for us as His children. Someone raised his hand and asked a question: "I don't think God loves us enough the way you claim. Why would you say God wants the best for us even though we do not experience it in our daily lives?"

To this the coach replied, "So you have a son, right?" The man answered yes, and the coach asked if he wanted his son to attain his highest potential on earth. The dad replied yes. The coach then asked the man if it was possible that his son might want to settle for less even though his father desired the highest level of growth and wellness for him, to which the man responded yes. Then the coach went on to explain how God wants the best life for his children, meaning he wants them to live to their fullest potential. But although this is what God wants for us, we also have to desire it for it to happen. Even though this is God's intention for us, we may end up settling for less than our highest potential on earth. We can choose a different path from what God has designed for us, and when that happens, only we bear the brunt.

I share this story to let you know that you're not doing God a favor when you choose to live a life of obedience to Him; you are actually doing yourself a favor, because when you make the deliberate choice to follow God's directives for your life, you are the one to benefit from your obedience. God wants only the best for you, and you will enjoy it if you make a deliberate choice to put God first by following His directives for your life lovingly.

You haven't lived on earth before, and so you are likely to make mistakes. This is your first attempt at living on Earth, but there is someone who made you . . . God! You are God's idea; therefore, you were intentionally created. You are not a biological accident. God had a purpose in mind when he thought about you. By becoming aware of that idea, you discover your purpose, and by seeking to partner with God and living your life according to that idea, you learn obedience. The human spirit was created to always seek a fuller and higher expression of itself.

God exists in the realm of abundance of resources, and He wants you to live in that realm as well. He wants you to walk in His abundance that's already made available.

I like to tell ladies, "You are fully resourced for what God has called you to be and do." So, when you find a lady acting contrary to her values, that is in disobedience to God's will for her life. That is often a clear indication that the lady is unaware of her life's purpose and the reason God created her, or that she is not fully aware that she is fully resourced by the Divine Creator (God). The third book of John 1:2 (NKJV) puts it best: "Beloved, I pray that you may prosper in all things and be in health, just as your soul prospers." This is what God wants for all His children, and staying in obedience to His word helps us receive this precious gift.

WHAT DOES OBEDIENCE TO GOD LOOK LIKE?

First, your belief drives your behavior. So, the first question, dear lady, is what do you believe? Do you believe God is your Father? Do you believe He loves you unconditionally? Now, I understand your background or life experiences may have conditioned you to believe that you are not loved by God. But you truly are.

Ephesians 2:10 (NIV) reads, "For we are God's handiwork, created in Christ Jesus to do good works, which God prepared in advance for us to do." This simply means obedience is not burdensome but rather a wonderful love relationship with the Lord.

The first book of John 5:3 (AMPC) reads, "For the [true] love of God is this: that we do His commands [keep His ordinances and are mindful of His precepts and teaching. And these orders of His are not irksome (burdensome, oppressive, or grievous." The message here is that God's commands are not meant to hurt us. They shouldn't be a burden, because his orders and laws are not oppressive or grievous. They actually are beautiful. Plus, He gives us the free will to make our decisions. So, when you choose to obey God, let it stem from a place of love, from a place that understands the genuine love of a Father.

I personally know people who, when God asked them to give up something they loved doing, wailed and cried about it because of how difficult it was to give up. Or they argue and argue or even outrightly disobey God because they feel they love it too much. And this amazes me. Loving God is such a sheer delight. Yes, sometimes it may not be convenient, but, again, the question becomes what is truly important to you.

SINGLENESS AS A GIFT

The season of being unmarried is such a blessed gift, and if you shift your perspective to see it as a gift, you will handle it differently.

Rather than look at singleness with dread, look at it like a season and seek to maximize it to the fullest. Obedience to God in this regard requires choosing to stay pure in a world filled with filth. Singleness should be seen as a gift to glorify God. It is also a time to draw near to God and dedicate yourself to discovering and living His purpose for your life.

Singleness should be seen as a beautiful time to grow and seek God's plan for your life. It is a time to walk in obedience to that plan even though the world makes single women feel like they are incomplete without a man. I want to remind you that your completeness is in God. Your single time is one of the only times you can give your undivided attention to God's service without any distractions. That's why Paul said in 1 Corinthians 7:32 that an unmarried person's concern is on how they can please the Lord. If you get married without finding your purpose and true calling, you may struggle to balance all that comes with marriage.

I find that some single ladies give God the barest minimum in obedience and service because they feel like they are too busy or they don't have that time. But your single years are actually a wonderful time to develop intimacy with God.

My mentor, a lady who married at the age of thirty-six, treated her single years as a gift. Her example helped me view my single years differently. I hope her story inspires you as well.

As a single lady, she used her skills to serve God. As a decorator, she undertook the task of decorating the church altar with beautiful decorations for church services, and she helped decorate the church during occasions like weddings and church programs. At times she would travel to interior villages to spread the gospel. A lot of the church members owed their walk with God to her because she went out into the streets to preach the gospel. One story that particularly stands out for me is how she was able to inspire and influence men to surrender to the Lord. She empowered them with teachings and prayers to build a solid walk with God, and she discipled them until they went from drunk men who were wasting away in clubs to solid kingdom financiers who were pillars of the church and kingdom projects.

So, you see, your singleness is not a curse but a gift you can use to serve the Lord with undivided attention.

The spirit of man seeks a higher and fuller expression of itself. Your single years are a time to draw closer to the Lord and to learn to discern His voice and follow His instructions. Discerning His voice will help you make the right decisions and choices. I find many people wait for marriage to hear God's voice or understand his leading in their marriage choice. But this should not be the case. Develop and discern the voice of God in your day-to-day interactions, the big and small decisions, and you will find that when it comes to marriage decisions, you will follow the same process to hear God's voice.

Your single years are such a beautiful opportunity to grow spiritually, obey God, and serve Him without the pressure and responsibilities of marriage. That is not to say married women cannot serve and obey God, but one should learn to flex and build those muscles of obedience while single. I recall that, as a single lady after university, I had a couple of months before my National Youth Service (a compulsory year of service to the country). There was a bit of a delay in getting my posting, so I had some time on my hands. I could've used that time to chill, watch movies, or party, but that would have been basically a waste of that time. My heart yearned for God, and I felt a leading in my heart to go to church like one would go to an office. I would be in church at 8:00 am and leave at 4:00 pm, and my plan was to read my Bible and pray and just press into God. People criticized me, saying that I was wasting my time in the church, but I have no regrets looking back. Those months were one of the best seasons of my life. It was a season of waiting on God. I read portions of scriptures, prayed, listened to sermons, and just basically served in church.

After I graduated from university, I dedicated an entire year to serving in NIFES (Nigerian Fellowship of Evangelical Students) as a volunteer. During that year, I visited over six universities and organized leadership training programs for student leaders, teaching and equipping them for service in their schools and helping them break free from limiting beliefs. All that was possible because I didn't have another human whose needs were directly or indirectly tied to me. Indeed, 1 Corinthians 7:34 (AMPC) says, "And the unmarried woman or girl is concerned and anxious about the matters of the Lord, how to be wholly separated and set apart in body and spirit; but the married woman has her cares [centered] in earthly affairs—how she may please her husband."

Sunday church services were another opportunity to serve. Services would start by 8:00 am, and church workers were expected to be in church at 7:30 am to pray for half an hour before service. I would go to church the previous evening and spend the night there with a friend. We would go to the sanctuary and talk about our walk with God, pray, and share scriptures before sleeping. In the morning, we would wake up early—by 5:30 am—to sweep the church, clean the bathrooms, dust the entire sanctuary, and set up the chairs before taking our baths and joining the other workers for the 7:30 am prayer meeting.

After church service, we would stay behind to assist our pastor and his wife. Then we would sweep, pack up the chairs, and be the last people to close the church gates.

Our service to God did not lessen our commitment to our parents and our other responsibilities. On Saturdays, we were not allowed to go to the church to sleep until we had done our chores and helped our parents prepare their Sunday meals.

Those were busy years, but they were also a beautiful time devoted completely to serving God. I have no regrets about those years. I encourage you to invest your single years in obedience and service to God. Just like the physical bank where you deposit your money, there is also a spiritual bank where you deposit your time, resources, and talent to God's kingdom. God never owes a man; the time will come when you need to withdraw from that reservoir of services to keep you going.

I also recall my undergrad years when we had so much time on our hands during semester breaks, and we would take time to just press into God, pray, fast, and seek God's face, and the outpouring of the Holy Spirit was so great. We had alumni/ae come to minister to us, and they would always advise us to maximize these times because we would not have the luxury of time when we graduated, started working, and perhaps got married. Oh, how right they were! Now, as a mom with three toddlers, I find that it often seems like twenty-four hours is not enough to do all that needs to be done in a day. And I do not have the luxury of time that I did in my undergraduate years.

At the moment, dear single lady, your single years are such a precious gift and an amazing time to serve God. Society may put pressure on you to 'settle down' or get a spouse. They may make you feel deficient and incomplete because you are not yet married. This pressure may come from your own family, parents and siblings, and even friends. They may make you feel like you are doing something wrong by being unmarried. I understand that this pressure can get to you, but please focus your attention on obeying God and trust that he will sort you out beautifully. Let God be your focus, and let pleasing Him be your goal. This will provide clarity and peace.

Obeying God as a single woman simply means aligning yourself with God's will for your life because obeying God should flow from a heart filled with love for God. I find that when you walk with God, He demands your all. Now, this begins little by little, and as you walk with Him and discover His love, you will want to go all out in loving Him and giving Him everything you are and have.

There is absolutely no disadvantage in obeying God. One example from biblical times of a woman who obeyed God is Mary, the mother of Jesus. She may have looked at her life as simple and insignificant, but heaven saw a heart that was yielded to God. Obedience first begins in the heart and yielding to God.

Some ladies say they love and obey God, but they are too lazy to get out of their comfort zones to pursue purpose. They are not involved in serving God, developing their potential, or adding value to themselves or other people around them. Yet they blame God for the fact that they are single. Some single ladies wear the badge of singleness as though God owes them.

Actually, nobody owes you anything. When you serve and obey God, don't do it with a sense of entitlement, but rather with a sense of gratitude to God for the gift of life and the desire to make a significant impact in the life of another . . . simply by being a difference maker, especially in a world where many are hurting.

How can you obey and serve God?

- The first way to obey and serve God is by adding value to yourself. You cannot give what you do not have. Do you have the right education, knowledge, and understanding to provide value to others? Have you come across people whom you know are typically carriers of value? What do their lives tell you? Do they point out the knowledge gap in your life? Now is the time to take action.
- Second, you must be willing to offer your body as a living sacrifice. Romans 12:1–2 (AMPC) says, "Therefore, I urge you, brothers and sisters, in view of God's mercy, to offer your bodies as a

living sacrifice, holy and pleasing to God—this is your true and proper worship. Do not conform to the pattern of this world, but be transformed by the renewing of your mind. Then you will be able to test and approve what God's will is—his good, pleasing and perfect will."

- The third way is by helping others. If you look around you, you will find someone in need. It might be in your workplace, your neighborhood, or your circle of friends. Serve others not because you want to be recognized or applauded by men, but because you genuinely want to make a difference and be a helping hand to others.

Obeying God as a single woman means stepping out of your comfort zone to do the things God wants you to do. Find out the needs around you, and allow yourself to become a difference maker. As Matthew 6:33 (AMPC) states, "But seek (aim at and strive after) first of all His kingdom and His righteousness (His way of doing and being right), and then all these things taken together will be given you besides."

Dear lady, your main priority is to seek God. Putting God first should be your priority because you are God's idea. He designed your life for a reason, and seeking Him first means aligning yourself with His will for your life. God has placed dreams and visions within us, and when you seek God first in whatever you do, you will find that you do not need to struggle to get other "things"; Matthew 6:33 says they will be added to you. Many of the things we seek are in fact add-ons; to seek them before seeking God is like putting the cart before the horse. Seeking God first means making sure your decisions and choices align with God's Word. Pray about your decisions and choices, such as what places to go, what jobs to accept, and what friendships to make. Putting God first means honoring those promises you make to yourself that please God, spending time in fellowship and communion, and spending time reading and meditating on God's Word.

The first book of Samuel 2:30 (CEV) reads: "I am the Lord, the God of Israel. I promised to always let your family serve me as priests, but now I tell you that I cannot do this any longer! I honor anyone who honors me, but I put a curse on anyone who hates me." If you honor God by putting Him first, He will honor you, but if you hate God with your choices and decisions, God says He will put a curse on you.

David is a man who honored God in the Bible, and God honored him. There are other examples of this in the Bible. Let's look at the life of Ruth. Ruth honored God by displaying loyalty to her mother-in-law, Naomi, and God honored her in return. Imagine a Moabite woman becoming the great-grandmother of King David. This could only happen in obedience and honor to God. Mary, the mother of Jesus, honored God and put Him first, and God honored her by choosing her to be the mother of Jesus. Both women put God first and walked in obedience, and God handpicked them for excellence and honor.

Let these biblical examples encourage and challenge you to put God first. He will elevate and honor you accordingly.

As a single lady, you have flexibility and freedom as you serve God wholeheartedly. I remember that, as a single undergraduate, I decided to stay back in school after my semester exams to just minister to people in prayers.

Here are some practical ways you can serve:

1. Volunteer your time in your church ministry or a ministry where you believe your skill set will make a difference. Or volunteer for community service.
2. Be a mentor or support to younger women who are still starting their spiritual journeys.
3. Join an outreach program to share the gospel or support mission work in your community or abroad.
4. Use your gifts, such as teaching, singing, writing, IT, organizing, etc., to contribute to the lives of people around you.
5. Organize prayer events and intercessory groups to intercede for others.
6. Embark on mission trips, whether long-term or short-term, to areas that would benefit from your support.

7. Support missionaries by praying for them, giving financially, or helping meet their practical needs.
8. Host gatherings or Bible studies in your home to foster fellowship and spiritual growth.
9. Serve in children's or youth ministries to help nurture the next generation in their faith.
10. Provide care and support for the less privileged or underserved communities.
11. Offer assistance to moms with newborns or toddlers, even for a couple of hours. This could be babysitting, helping with meals, cleaning their homes, etc. I remember when I had my third child, and a kind woman came over to help with my laundry. This gave me so much relief that I still appreciate to this date. Some came to hold the baby for some time to allow me time to rest while others prepared meals. These are services that a new mom would never forget.
12. Help seniors with their needs, such as mowing their lawns, packing snow, and helping with their grocery shopping.

Serving others doesn't always involve money. If you have time, invest it in the lives of others and watch the ripple effect. There are always three ways to invest: money, time and prayers. Choose the one that you can do and run with it.

Obey God in your everyday decisions. For example:

1. Honor God by staying pure with your body. "Do you not know that your body is the temple (the very sanctuary) of the Holy Spirit Who lives within you, Whom you have received [as a Gift] from God? You are not your own" (1 Corinthians 6:19–20). Sexual temptation is real and may present itself to you, but this is where your obedience is tested; you can either choose to honor God or give in to an immoral life. Food is another area where we are sometimes challenged to treat our bodies well. I recall when I wanted to lose weight, I had to put

away every form of food that would have tempted me to ditch my weight loss goal. I learned to eat in moderation by joining a support group where I was held accountable daily for the food choices I made. The same principles apply to resisting sexual temptations. It all begins in the mind and having someone who will hold you accountable. It could be your parents, friends, or a spiritual leader.

2. Manage your finances in a way that glorifies God, and give generously. Be a faithful tither. Give to projects that align with your passion, vision, and calling. Support God's work while at the same time learning how to manage your own finances by saving and investing. As a board-certified financial professional, I have helped many people save more and make prudent investments that grew their wealth. The more wealth you have, the more you can contribute to the kingdom of God.

3. Choose relationships that align with God's will. Chemistry is real, and sometimes we can get so fired up by TDH (tall, dark, and handsome) that we go against our own convictions about honoring God with our relationships.

I encourage you to take these practical steps. Start by picking a day of the week to just fast and pray and wait on God for guidance and direction. Get a journal if you do not already have one, and use it to write down whatever God lays in your heart. Find a quiet time daily to pray, worship, read the scriptures, and just meditate on what you have read. Sit in silence to listen to God's voice. Do these things daily, and you will find that your walk with God deepens.

CHALLENGES TO OBEDIENCE AND SERVICE

Have you ever made a decision to fast and then, all of a sudden, the hunger pangs you feel that particular day seem like they were sent to finish your life? This challenge of the flesh warring against the spirit is real, and I understand.

You will face many challenges to obedience and service, and I want you to know that they are not uncommon. I understand these struggles. Struggles like:

1. Impatience and discontentment with being single.
2. Societal expectations and pressure to prioritize things that do not glorify God.
3. Self-doubt and fear of stepping out in faith because we may lack validation from those we love and respect.

These are all common struggles we face as Christians. Here are some ways to overcome them:

1. The right community is everything! And by community, I do not necessarily mean a lot of people. Your community could be one or two persons. Regardless, pray for and seek out a solid team of people who love, respect and believe in you.
2. Spend time with God to help you renew your mind. Read books that inspire and challenge you. Trust God's timing as you wait.
3. Learn to have fun and enjoy your life while you wait. Don't put your life on hold because you are waiting or because you are obedient.

WHAT ARE SOME BENEFITS OF OBEYING AND SERVING GOD?

You are God's idea, and when you live a life of obedience and service aligned with God, you experience a deep spiritual contentment. This happens when you know you are right in the center of God's will, doing precisely what you know He wants you to do at each moment.

Emotionally and relationally, there is joy and peace in living beyond yourself and making a difference in someone else's life.

1. You draw closer to God as you understand God's purpose for your life. Nothing compares to enjoying deep communion with the Father.
2. Through obedience and service, you develop your own character and become a better version of yourself. Character traits like patience, humility, and perseverance are priceless qualities you will develop.
3. When a single lady obeys and serves God, she experiences completeness, peace, and joy.

I recall I once asked my friend to go to the university and evangelize with me. She wanted us to go have our photos taken instead. Eventually, she set aside the idea of a photo shoot and went with me to preach the gospel on campus. We were actually very dressed up for that evangelism because we wanted to catch the attention of the university students. And we did. We shared the gospel with some of the students, and just as we were leaving, we noticed a young man taking pictures of us from afar. We spoke with him, and it turned out he had just gotten a new camera and was trying it out. We looked at his photos and realized he had taken some good shots of us while we walked. So, we asked him for a proper photoshoot, and we got two in one! These were very beautiful pictures from a professional photographer, plus evangelism and winning souls for the Lord. This reminds me of Matthew 6:33. If you seek God's kingdom first, every other thing will be added to you.

HOW TO PREPARE FOR MARRIAGE THROUGH OBEDIENCE AND SERVICE

When you focus on becoming the woman God wants you to be, you will find that you become a better version of yourself and a better spouse. Learning to trust the Lord and to walk with Him will help you cultivate trust in your future spouse and understand how to adapt to him.

Cultivating your relationship with the Lord will also help you live a selfless life. Selflessness is definitely needed in marriage because it's a time of service—a time of living not for yourself but for your family. You will have to learn to cater to the needs of your family.

Reflection

I want you to reflect on your choices and actions and ask yourself these questions:

- Are you currently serving the Lord with your gifts and skills?
- What distractions are keeping you from giving the Lord your all?
- What can you do about the distractions?

Create time with the Lord daily during which you pray, read Scripture, and meditate on God's word. Look around you at opportunities to serve God in your church or community. Seek God's face to guide you in your decisions and choices. May God meet you in the place of your obedience.

CHAPTER 10
How to Identify Your King

The world we live in today is filled with frustrated females who are living with men who aren't going anywhere. If you are a single man reading this chapter, you must decide not to join that statistic. It's ridiculous for a man to ask a woman to leave her parents' home to follow him when he isn't going anywhere.

The first question a lady should ask a man who asks her to follow him is: "Where are you going in life?" If he can't answer this question, you should ask him to find a map and call you when he has more clarity. Dear single lady, you are too precious to waste your life sitting at home for years, frustrated.

So many awesome women are being suffocated by men who don't know what they are doing. God says, "I created her to adapt to the male." The male has to have something for her to adapt to. Permit me to remind you that you are powerful, and God's plan for you is His best. As a woman, you are wired to submit, but you should truly submit only when you recognize that the man you are about to submit to knows where he is going.

Truly, God has designed women to be adaptable. But you must remember that some men don't deserve to be adapted to. They are not worthy of it. They're not giving the adapter a comfortable position to adapt to. When this is the case, you will find women adapting in bitterness, hatred, deceit, or malice, as if they have been forced against their wills to adapt. But this isn't the will of God for you, my dear woman. This is why I remind you: refuse to settle for less than God's best for you.

There are people who will undermine you, what you do, and who you are. And that's okay. Stay away from them and spend time with people who encourage you, inspire you, and celebrate you.

Stay in the positive energy zone. This is you developing stress resilience.

I am taking the time to explain all these to give you a balanced view on how to identify the man who is right for you. More often than not, women make decisions about marriage based on how they feel. But the man makes decision of marriage by checking off boxes of things he wants.

For instance, ask a woman why she wants to marry a man, and she will tell you that it's because of how he makes her feel. When you ask the man why he wants to marry this woman, he will usually say it's because she is this and that and has this and that . . . very specific qualities or attributes he is looking out for.

Here is an example. A man takes a woman out for dinner. During the conversation, she blushes at how he looks at her, his command of English, and how he makes her laugh. The woman goes home and tells her family and friends about the ambiance of the restaurant, the taste of the cocktail, and the fragrance the man wore or even how he looked.

Meanwhile, during this same dinner date, if the man is a focused man, he asks the woman specific questions about things like her job, her background, and her culinary skills with the goal of assessing her intellectual capacity and checking out her nurturing skills.

I understand the above example may not apply to every woman and man, but the point is that men are built and designed to be logical, while women are adaptable, emotional, and moved by environmental stimuli. Hence they have different perspectives. This is why you must cultivate spiritual sensitivity as a single woman and allow the Lord to lead you in identifying your king.

I always advise a coffee chat, lunch, or casual stroll for the first-time meetup. You do not want to commit yourself to a three-course, two-hour dinner with someone and be stuck when you realize five minutes in, he's a forty-year-old aspiring rapper. No, I'm not mean; I'm just realistic.

It's also the truth. Remember the truth will set you free. Also remember to dress your authentic self. Some ladies spend unbelievable hours preparing for lunch or coffee dates. I'm not saying you shouldn't look your best, but keep it real and look your beautiful self at the same time.

Dear woman, your essence is love. When God made the woman, He drew her out of man so that the man would have someone to love who was of his own nature. It was love that brought about the woman's existence. The man was created to be a giver of love and the woman to be a receiver of love. The primary purpose of the female's receiving nature is to receive love. In Ephesians 5:25 (NIV), Paul says, "Husbands, love your wives, just as Christ loved the church and gave himself up for her." He repeats this again in verse 28 when he says, "In this same way, husbands ought to love their wives as their own bodies. He who loves his wife loves himself" (Ephesians 5:28 NIV). And in verse 33 of the same chapter, he concludes by saying, "Each one of you also must love his wife as he loves himself" (Ephesians 5:33 NIV).

A friend of mine shared how she and her ex-husband used to fast and pray during courtship, and they had answers to their prayers. Some days, he would ask for them to pray together. So, she believed this man was born again because none of the men she had dated in the past had ever encouraged her to fast, let alone suggest that they do it together. So she believed this man loved God and was the right man for her.

After they separated and she was sharing this story with me, I asked further questions about the relationship before marriage. It turned out there were glaring red flags that she had ignored. She ignored them because she believed fasting and prayer were a big deal and testament to his godliness. She felt like she was probably blowing his faults out of proportion. But this is where we get things wrong. That a man fasts and prays doesn't make him right for us. We must look at his service, and, beyond that, into his character. When all is said and done in church, you will live with the man and do life with him.

The purpose of something can be found only in the mind of its maker. Men therefore need a God-given identity if they are to fulfill their true purpose. We must learn what God originally intended for them. To do this, we must go back and rediscover the Creator's original plan for both men and women. Over the years, society has made a man define his identity by his roles. But being a man is far more than traditionally defined roles. There is a core identity rooted in who the Creator designed him to be. A man's identity is found in his purpose, not in his roles. What happens is the moment his role changes, he becomes confused because he loses the basis for his manhood.

Once more, we must realize that when men are ignorant of their true identity, it affects not only their own callings and fulfillment but also those of their families and of society as a whole. This is because God has given males a unique leadership influence. As the man goes, so goes the family, society, and his world.

With those things in mind, dear lady, please ask yourself these pertinent questions when making your choice of a husband:

- Does he define his worth based on God's purpose, rather than society's roles?
- Has he learned about God's vision for his life?
- Is he living in the truth of who he is created to be?

When a man understands the purpose and responsibilities God has given him and the true design of his relationship with his woman, he can be free to fulfill their destiny and potential. He can be the man he was created to be.

Dear lady, you must begin to notice narcissistic men, men who subconsciously see women as less than themselves. You'll hear it in their words and see it in their actions. This is a sign you definitely don't want to ignore. Maybe he treats you as very special, but if he treats other women in his life like trash, one day it will be your turn. Such men will be intimidated by your success. They can even go as far as hitting you, putting you down, or speaking demeaning words to reduce your self-worth. In the church setting, they may pray and fast and seem very spiritual; people may genuinely admire them. But a man's upbringing has the upper hand in his daily life, and if he has unhealed wounds left over from his upbringing, his character outside of church may be inconsistent with his prayers. To such men, women are conquests. They conquer one woman and move on to the next woman. Study the man thoroughly to be sure he doesn't exhibit these tendencies. Such a man is definitely not your king. A lady looking for her king must ensure that she has an authority figure over her. This is usually your parents, but if your parents have passed on, you must find other people who can represent the role of your parents in your life so the man knows you come with your own support. If not, you may suffer in the hands of a man who sees women as disposable and lesser than himself.

Some men, through no fault of their own, have no understanding of what marriage is. How, then, can these men know what a beautiful marriage looks like? How can they learn to speak the right words over their women? There is a great divide between the good men and bad men. Some men have never seen their father treat their mother like the queen she is, so they treat the woman in their life like a stranger instead of a wife because this is what they have been taught. That is why you must ask these important questions:

- Who was your father?
- Who taught you what fatherhood is?
- Who are your role models for what it means to be a good man?
- Who was your role model's father, and what example did he set?

You had best believe that unless a man is intentional, he'll replicate and even multiply what he learned passively and actively. The man is the bridegroom. Part of his role is to trim the edges of his garden, which is the woman. Many people preach marriage from the standpoint of tradition instead of the Word of God. In our mothers' time, many women didn't go to school, but today, girls are high flyers in their jobs. Some men feel threatened by a woman who earns money because they think it denies them their perceived traditional role of being the provider for their family. A man who doesn't understand the spiritual dynamics of marriage will struggle to support you as you grow in your career and as a spiritual woman. Both parties will have to make a lot of mindset changes for the good of being able to support one another, but if the man is not ready to play his part, then maybe he is not the right one for you.

Asides from asking these vital questions, you also want to be certain your values align with a man's before you allow yourself to get emotionally involved with him. Oftentimes, ladies get swept away by a man's looks or even by his deep chocolate voice. I call this the TDH Effect (tall, dark, and handsome) or the BBE Effect (broad-shouldered, blue-eyed). But when the chips are down in the marriage and real issues come up—like holding the baby at night so you can catch some desperately needed sleep, speaking to you kindly during an argument, or understanding what's happening to you and helping out—you will not think of how chocolate his voice is or how broad his shoulders are. His core values and character will become more important at that point. This is not to say a man or woman should not care about their physical presentation, but beyond that surface there are more things that should be looked at.

The devil hates godly marriages and godly homes and will do anything to twist God's plan. He goes all the way into the childhood of a man or woman and manipulates their environment, their parents' marriage, etc., to twist their perceptions and their reality so they start believing the wrong things. The man ends up seeing a woman as a threat or someone who is good only for making babies, which is why some men cannot stand real women. A real woman is clothed with grace and anointing, knows where she is going, and is ready to help. So, if you are a real woman, watch out for the following red flags in a man. Is your man uncomfortable with your success and achievements? Does he feel threatened by all you come with? Does he talk down to you, bully you, or ignore and resist your attempts to help? If yes, it's time to walk away so you do not get trapped in a marriage that will stifle your creativity and limit your productivity. In identifying your king, you must be aware of the telltale signs that a relationship is headed for the rocks.

RED FLAGS

Some men are in church for business—specifically, the business of marrying a potential moneybag or sex toy. Watch for the red flags that indicate this kind of man. Red flags mean STOP. Watch your step. Do not enter. Abort mission.

Dear lady, what are some red flags to watch out for?

1. Dishonesty. His words and actions are questionable. You see loopholes in his words and actions.
2. Trust issues. Trust is the bedrock of a thriving marriage. If you are not yet married and you already don't trust him because he is still loving his ex or doing shady things, that is a bad sign.
3. Disrespect. There should be mutual respect in a relationship, but if you have seen repeated signs of disrespect, RUN. It doesn't matter if he is doing a hundred-day fast. RUN.
4. Uncontrolled temper. If he beats you up or curses you out when he is angry, that is an abusive man. There is no excuse for abuse.
5. Immaturity. If he doesn't know how to manage his emotions—if he throws tantrums or holds grudges, for example—my dear sister, RUN.
6. Laziness. A man by nature is a provider and protector of his wife and children. So, if he constantly has excuses for why he is not a provider, or if he's always borrowing money from you or depending on you to feed him during the relationship . . . RUN.
7. Addictions. Whether the addiction is to drugs, smoking, alcohol, gambling, his phone, or anything else, a man dealing with addiction who is not ready to seek help isn't ready for marriage. You must step back because you are about to get married to a liability.
8. Infidelity of any sort.
9. Gossip.
10. No relational skills. Ask him about his friends. If he can't keep or maintain friendships, there may be a problem.

There are so many more red flags, but I pray that the Holy Spirit will help you identify them and help you get out before it is too late. Sometimes it takes a while to get to know people, and as you peel the layers back, you discover some things that need to be flagged. Some women see these red flags and decide to wait to see just how red the flag is. This is a bad idea. A red flag is a red flag. If something is nonnegotiable for you, a little of it should be no more acceptable than a lot of it.

In fact, go ahead now and create your own list of red flags. Please show it to a solid mentor or a trusted and wise friend as well.

Reflection

The number one criterion you should look out for in a man is one who fears God. I do not mean simply a nice man, or a man who goes to church, but a man who has a walk with the Lord. The opposite of all the red flags we identified are qualities to look out for in a man you want to spend the rest of your life with:

- A man who is honest and transparent with you.
- A man who respects you and shares your values.
- A man who is emotionally stable and mature with whom you can resolve conflicts.
- A man with clearly defined boundaries with the opposite sex. He knows where to draw the line in his relationships and communications with you and other women.
- A man who has self-control and does not need the influence of substances or devices to stay level-headed. Some people, including women, have become addicted to their devices (phones, tablets, etc.) and are on medication because they have told themselves they are suffering from ADHD when, in a very real sense, they are addicted to their devices.

I like to emphasize that while you are looking out for dealbreakers, do not become, to borrow the words of Isaiah 54:17, a weapon formed against yourself that will prosper.

If you're constantly conforming when you meet someone new, it's a red flag. It means you don't really know yourself and the core values that are important to you. Too many people get into relationships and get lost in the other person. You date an attorney, now you're watching reruns of *Suits* every night. You date a preacher, now you're in church at every service. This is not to say you shouldn't learn to adapt, but please don't adapt and lose yourself or become a chameleon who is always adapting like crazy because you want a ring on your finger.

If you find any of these dealbreakers in your own character, it's time to pause and work on yourself, because you cannot give what you don't have. You cannot be lazy and be searching for a hard-working man. For a responsible man who fears God, laziness is a red flag that he needs to avoid. Ask yourself this question: what do I need to work on to be the ideal woman? Then use this chapter as a guide when men come to you.

CHAPTER 11

Nurturing Your Relationship in Preparation for Marriage

Now that you have eliminated dealbreakers and red flags and want to take things a step further toward marriage, let's look at how to nurture a relationship from dating or courtship to marriage. This chapter is for when you identify someone you think you want to spend the rest of your life with. You now want to nurture that relationship in ways that will lead to the best possible marriage. To nurture means to care for and encourage the growth or development of something or someone. Nurturing your relationship is, therefore, cultivating your relationship with your fiancé to ensure you have a good foundation for your marriage.

ESTABLISH BOUNDARIES

The first item on your marriage preparation checklist is establishing boundaries.

I want to share the story of Jim and Fanny with you. This couple had their first session with a marriage counselor one year into their marriage. As soon as the conversation started, they started to hurl blame at one another. Jim said his bride was controlling, and he was tired of her controlling ways. The counselor asked the wife if she thought her husband's accusations were true. In her defense, Fanny explained that her husband was secretive and never shared anything with her. She went on to say that he was very insensitive and unkind when relating with her. The counselor then asked Jim if his wife's accusations were true. Jim responded that Fanny had zero respect when speaking to him and that he always needed to speak to her harshly to get her out of his space.

This argument went on for the duration of their session.

Now, you may be wondering: This was just one year into the marriage—how did things deteriorate so fast? The answer is responsibility. Did you notice how both Jim and Fanny did not take responsibility for their individual actions? Rather, they each blamed the other person for their actions. For love to work, you and your partner have to realize your freedom, and the way to know this is by defining your boundaries—what freedoms you have and don't have.

Dear lady, once you are certain of the man you want to spend the rest of your life with, each of you will need to take responsibility for making the relationship work and building one another up. Building a relationship that leads to marriage is not the work of only the woman, as some cultures and traditions put it. It takes two to tango. Both the man and the woman must be willing to learn to build a lasting relationship. I see many ladies who, the moment a man proposes, swing into action and begin to act like the wife, cooking for him, cleaning his house, doing his laundry, basically playing wife in the hope that he will be impressed enough to want to walk down the aisle with her as soon as possible.

Dear lady, *you* are the prize. The Bible says that a man who finds a wife finds a good thing and obtains favor from God. The man who finds you has found a good thing and should be thankful for the gift of you—and vice versa, of course, but do not throw yourself at the man and go out of your way to keep him.

That is where the basic principle of sowing and reaping comes in— setting healthy boundaries as you plan for your wedding and marriage.

This is the season to build your friendship with one another and incorporate boundaries as you get to know one another more. This happens through conversations and engaging in activities that help you understand yourselves. You can engage in community service, go on dates, and spend time with each other's family and friends.

As you spend time together, dear lady, please learn to ask the right questions, it'll help you decide if this relationship is worth making into a lifelong commitment. Some questions to ask are:

1. What are you most excited about in your life right now?
2. Where do you see yourself in ten years?
3. Do you consider yourself healed from past traumas?
4. What are your religious or spiritual beliefs?
5. What are some of your biggest fears?
6. Who do you look up to the most?
7. What do you consider to be the roles of a husband and a wife?
8. What are you like when you're angry? How do you handle disagreements?

These questions will help you learn more about this person and create needed boundaries. God designed the entirety of creation for freedom. We were not meant to be enslaved by each other but to love each other freely. God designed us to have freedom of choice as we respond to life, other people, God, and ourselves. But when we turned from God, we lost our freedom. We became enslaved to sin, to self-centeredness, to other people, to guilt, and to a whole host of other dynamics. Boundaries help us to realize our freedom once again. Listen to the way that Paul tells the Galatians to set boundaries against any type of control and become free: "In [this] freedom Christ has made us free [and completely liberated us]; stand fast then, and do not be hampered and held ensnared and submit again to a yoke of slavery [which you have once put off]" (Galatians 5:1 NASB). Boundaries make love grow because each one is free to choose to be him- or herself and to love.

Marriage is not slavery. It is based on a love relationship deeply rooted in freedom. Each partner is free from the other and, therefore, free to love the other. Where there is control, or the perception of control, there is no love. Love exists only where there is freedom. Now is the time to understand each other's boundaries and create healthy boundaries that'll help you thrive as individuals and as a couple.

In understanding each other, I encourage you not to spend forever getting to know yourselves; set a timeline. It would benefit you to have someone in your life with whom you can speak freely about your relationship and receive wise counsel and support for the journey.

Now is also the time to get a marriage counselor to help you navigate conversations around building the foundation for a healthy marriage. Conversations on finance, communication, sex, etc., can make or break a home. And since it will take both parties to build the marriage, it's highly important to start right.

Attend marriage seminars together, read books together, and listen to sermons and other personal growth or career-building topics and teachings together. This will help you understand one another. Always remember that you come from different backgrounds and have different ways of seeing issues and doing things.

After spending time together, ask yourself these questions:

1. How did I feel in his company?
2. What did I learn about him and his character?
3. What am I going to do with the information I have now?

Remember our reflection and introspection from Chapter 2? Now is the time to apply these principles.

Let me tell you the story of Emmanuel and Emily. They were in love with each other and were thoroughly convinced they were meant for each other. They spent their courtship days dining out and having a beautiful time but avoiding hard conversations that strained their sweet times. Upon getting married, they faced those real issues they hadn't wanted to discuss earlier. This was when they found out their values were completely different. Gradually, communication declined until they both walked away from the marriage because they believed they were too different from each other and there was simply no understanding.

What do you notice here? The honeymoon phase of their relationship waned, and they entered the reality phase, which happens to every couple. But because they had not intentionally built structures to prepare for the reality phase, their relationship couldn't withstand the pressure of everyday life, and they weren't ready to fight for their marriage. They both chose the easy way out: divorce or separation. In some other cases, one person may end up enduring or taking on the consequences of the other spouse's bad behavior.

The earth operates by laws. I want to discuss two of them.

The law of sowing and reaping says that what you sow, so shall you reap, and this law applies even to marriage relationships. Your dating and courtship season is the time to take responsibility for learning to be a no-drama partner and put in the work to sow the seeds of a healthy marriage.

The law of relationships means that you are responsible *to* your spouse but you are not responsible *for* your spouse. Some adults have not learned to grow up and act responsibly. They were raised in environments that enabled bad character, and now they are about to carry on their bad character into their marriage.

Dear lady, please understand this: there are things you have power over and things you have no control or power over.

First, let's talk about what we don't have power over. We have no power over the attitudes and actions of other people. We can't make our partners grow up. We can't stop another human being from exhibiting a troublesome habit or character flaw, such as yelling at a partner or giving her the silent treatment. The fruit of the Spirit is self-control, not control by another (Galatians 5:23). God himself does not exercise such power over us, even though he could (2 Peter 3:9).

So, as you nurture your relationship, watch out that you do not become an enabler of bad character. If you notice some character traits you are not comfortable with, now is the time to talk about them. If he is ready to change and makes adjustments, you may continue, but if there are things you notice as dealbreakers, now is the time to evaluate whether to continue or walk away. A broken engagement is better than a broken marriage.

If you come from a family with controlling or abusive parent(s), you may not know how to draw the line of respect in a healthy relationship. You may even be the controlling person.

Let me tell you the story of Brian and Julie. Brian complained, "Sometimes Julie withdraws from me for no reason at all." Julie replied that there was a reason: she withdrew when she tried to say no to him and he tried to control her. Brian was shocked to hear this. He felt he didn't try to control her when she said no. Julie, not wanting to argue, let it go and instead said, "I guess we have a difference of opinion." Later that evening, Brian invited a friend over to watch a ball game. His friend checked his schedule and said, "Sorry, I can't." Brian threw up his arms in mock exasperation and said, "Oh, come on, you can go! Just rearrange things a little." Brian's wife, Julie, observed this exchange and said, "That's it; that's the way you try to control me." Brian was surprised to hear this.

What do you notice from this story? Brian was not used to people saying no to him, so he tried to control the person or the situation, which is very unhealthy for any relationship and uncomfortable for the partner. Dear lady, please check yourself. Does this describe the man you are thinking of marrying? Does it describe you? If you say yes to either of those questions, now is the time for the controlling person in the relationship to work on making adjustments.

As I often say: that all families on earth are dysfunctional, but some are more dysfunctional than others. Some marriages and families are so unhealthy it is painful to watch. What if your parents set an example of extreme dysfunction and you haven't yet learned to manage your emotions or handle delicate relationships such as marriage? Now is the time to begin to work on you, and you should do so with the same intentionality you use to work on your relationship. No one but you will do the work.

How do you even know if you are controlling? Ask your family and friends to answer these questions for you:

- Have I been crossing your boundaries?
- When you say no to me, do you feel I respect your decision?
- Do I guilt-trip you, withdraw, or attack you when you set a limit?
- Will you let me know the next time I don't respect your freedom?

These humbling and uncomfortable questions show you are willing to grow. Candid answers from your loved ones will help you grow and become better. Remember that discomfort can sometimes be an opportunity for growth.

How do you access growth? By the measure of changes and improvement in quality of life. How do you know something is living? If it's growing. So as long as we are living, we must continue to make positive changes to improve our quality of life and that of others around us. Your relationship phase is a time of growing. And by growth, I mean that you learn, unlearn, and re-learn. Marriage is a melting pot where two individuals come together to make a living and build a single-family unit. It is a delicate relationship where you have to constantly choose growth.

As you work on yourself, do not neglect setting limits in your relationship because of a fear of causing pain. Pain can be the best friend your relationship has ever had. Remember, the early phase is the honeymoon phase, where you both see eye to eye on a lot of things. If you confront painful discussions instead of avoiding them, you will have a solid foundation that you can continue to improve on when the honeymoon phase passes and reality sets in.

PROACTIVE BOUNDARIES

When conflict arises, it is better to set the needed boundary immediately than to let the issue slide. This is called setting proactive boundaries. Couples who set proactive boundaries look like they are always having conflicts, but this is how they are able to lay a foundation quickly and set limits for what each person wants or doesn't want.

Roy and Stacy are a good example of the importance of proactive boundaries. Roy loves Stacy, and he can't wait to marry her. She comes from a family where she suffered poverty, lack, and deprivation; life was hard for her growing up. Roy has vowed to be her shield and protect and provide for her as much as he can. Stacy, though, is very manipulative, a character trait she picked up as a child since it helped her get away with consequences and find ways around people and situations. During the honeymoon phase of their relationship, Roy didn't notice

Stacy's manipulative tendencies because even though she was manipulative, she was also sweet and soft-spoken. Increasingly, Roy notices her manipulations, but she covered them up with her sweetness, and he feels guilty about confronting her or trying to correct her.

What do you think will happen if Roy does not have a sit-down conversation with Stacy to state his boundaries clearly? When the reality phase begins, he may blow like a fuse. From my work as a DISC (Dominance, Influence, Steadiness, and Conscientiousness) consultant, I know that some people have easygoing, compliant personalities, but when pushed to their limit, they will erupt and the results are not pretty. It is not good when one partner in a relationship is always the one who gives in. Even if the one who concedes seems content with that role, that may change when the honeymoon phase of the relationship is over.

ADD VALUE TO YOURSELF

The next item on your marriage preparation checklist is adding value to yourself. Dear lady, now is the time to grow you as well as the relationship. Real growth is intentional. When you were a child, you probably didn't even realize when you grew up, except for when people commented on your height, how developed you had become, or when a favorite dress no longer fit. When you become an adult, finish your education, and maybe get a job, growth no longer happens automatically; you have to be deliberate about it. I recall when I quit my last job and took some time away from the working world to care for my children. During this time, I knew it was about time that I become an entrepreneur and launch my own business. I had to go through a period of self-discovery again because I had changed, and my life had changed. I now had children I was responsible to and responsible for. I had a spouse. I couldn't continue the way I had been; I had to grow and re-discover myself, because you cannot give what you don't have. It was during this period that I opened the door to things I could control. I took responsibility for my life actions. When you cease to blame other people and instead own your problems, you are then empowered to make changes to solve your problems.

This, dear lady, is the secret to personal growth and changing your life forever. You are not a victim. If you continue to think and act like life happens to you, you will continue to blame others. Personal growth here also implies setting limits on yourself, providing a context in which you can grow. This is extremely important, because when you do this for yourself, you can apply the same principle in a marriage relationship.

Why should we become responsible for our own growth? The Bible explains it clearly in Matthew 7:5 (NIV): "First take the plank out of your own eye, and then you will see clearly to remove the speck from your brother's eye." Before you begin to set limits in your relationship with another human being, you need to take responsibility for your heart, your love, your time, and your talents. We are to own our lives and live in God's light, growing up and maturing our characters along the way: "[S]peaking the truth in love, we will grow to become in every respect the mature body of him who is the head, that is, Christ" (Ephesians 4:15 NIV). This is our job and no one else's.

Dear lady, are you aware that while we are only partly responsible for growing our marriages, we are completely responsible to God for developing our very souls? Yes, the Bible says, "For we must all appear before the judgment seat of Christ, that each one may receive what is due us for the things done while in the body, whether good or bad" (2 Corinthians 5:10 NIV).

Why do I emphasize the need to grow you? Because when you set limits on yourself, you create an environment in which your spouse and the people in your life can become free to choose and grow. While some of us are passive, others are reactive, and so it's important to evaluate your current self. It might be painful to admit that there is something about you that needs improving, but it's for the best.

Part of growing you is having your own income. I like to say: 'I love you' doesn't pay bills." Take the time to add value to yourself because you cannot give what you don't have. Add value to yourself by learning a trade, starting a business, getting an education, having a job, and otherwise engaging in personal development.

BE AN AVID READER

Reading books is an essential item for your marriage preparation checklist.

It's interesting how some people stop reading books the moment they graduate from high school or university. Learning is a lifelong journey, and there are many things competing with books for our attention in today's social-media-saturated world. Reading a book has to be an intentional activity, for reading is the best way to grow and develop into the woman you were called to be. You can advance your own career by reading books in your field, but do not make the mistake of focusing only on your own interests. When you read a good book on marriage, how to develop your mind, etc., you can share it with your partner and develop similar interests, strengthening your bond.

Before my husband and I got married, I recommended books I had read or was looking forward to reading, and we would pace ourselves and read those books together. These books became fodder for conversation. A reader is a leader.

SEEK CHRISTIAN PREMARITAL COUNSELING

In addition to reading books about marriage, my future husband and I also had premarital counseling sessions with our pastor. This counseling greatly helped us by showing us things we needed to address and talk about before moving to marriage. I highly recommend premarital counseling by a trained, experienced Christian counselor to help you navigate certain conversations and build a strong foundation for communication, especially since both of you come from two different backgrounds, have different personalities and have varying opinions about the various aspects of marriage.

HAVE MARRIAGE MENTORS

Whatever age you might be or whatever your social status, have a spirit-filled, mature married couple with whom you can speak and pray in your marital journey.

A mentor I respected very much as a teenager told me she had gotten married without knowing much about navigating the first few years of marriage. She was a preacher, and many people sought her counsel regarding marital issues, so she did not expect to have difficulty navigating her own marriage. These expectations were dashed when the first year of their marriage was very rough. Because she was a preacher, her husband assumed she knew what to do, and so did everyone else. As a result, when they had disagreements and conflicts, she had no one to speak to. I encourage you to save yourself from the heartache of these situations by having a mature, married Christian couple you can talk and pray with about marriage.

Amanda had been married for a couple of years when she noticed her husband was beginning to act strangely. He was spending more time on his phone than usual, shutting her out of his life by not engaging in conversations, and picking fights unnecessarily. She confided in a godly woman from her church, and they agreed to pray every night for half an hour. Amanda was angry, but this woman encouraged her to continue to walk in love regardless. In the place of prayers, the Lord revealed that Amanda's husband was getting involved with another woman. With prayers, that relationship was broken. Amanda's husband got into a terrible fight with the other woman, then came back to his wife, confessed his wrongdoing, and apologized for the hurt he'd caused. This is an abridged version of the story, but you see the point: If Amanda had approached the matter by herself, things might have gotten really messy because she was ready to go to great lengths to hurt him and she might have done something really crazy. This shows the wisdom of seeking godly counsel.

You must also commit to growing and building the right relationships. I encourage women not to isolate. Surround yourself with wise women and wise support groups that can gently but firmly help you see areas where you need to grow. It's a circle that'll love you deeply enough to confront your shenanigans gently.

Surrounding yourself with godly friends is enriching and mutually beneficial to both of you. And if you do not have such friends, begin to pray about it right now. A friend of mine shared how she and her husband prayed for godly friends they could go on vacations with and hang out with. Most importantly, they prayed for friends with whom they shared the same values. A couple of months later, that prayer was answered. They were introduced to another couple and their friendship was so organic, and their new friends introduced them to another couple who were their friends also. The interesting part was how the children of all three couples were in the same age bracket. They went on vacations and fellowships together. The night before the end of their first group vacation, they spent the evening praying together, and there was an interplay of spiritual gifts through the word of knowledge and prophecies. My dear lady in waiting, don't do life in isolation!

Reflection

A man ought to have another person he respects, honors and listens to. For some men, it's their biological dad. For others, it's their pastor or their boss at work. Do not submit to a man who does not have an authority figure over him—a man whom he submits to, whose voice he respects. The reason for this is: God made the man to be the head of the home, and when he submits to a higher authority, it helps bring a balanced view in certain grey areas that may arise in the future as he navigates family life. Plus, it helps him maintain boundaries and listen to advice at times when he needs a voice of reason and counsel other than yours.

Married life has varying seasons; through each season, your decisions and choices will either make or mar your lives forever. This is why surrounding yourselves intentionally with friends with whom you share the same values is paramount. Pray to have these kinds of relationships if you do not already have them—godly men as friends for your husband, and godly women as friends for yourself. God created us as social beings.

CHAPTER 12
The Feminine Woman and How to Be Soft

The word *feminine* has been abused. Over the years, culture and tradition have defined femininity to mean different things. In fact, when some people hear the word *femininity*, they think of a weak person, as though being feminine is the same as being weak. Hence, you find tomboys—girls who act boyish or carry themselves as tough and strong to protect themselves from harm.

But what is the true definition of femininity? Femininity is your identity in Christ as a woman. To help you understand fully, let's briefly see how the woman came about in the first place. This will provide context for our femininity.

The Bible says in Genesis 2:21–22 (NIV) that "the Lord God caused the man to fall into a deep sleep; and while he was sleeping, he took one of the man's ribs and closed up the place with flesh. Then the Lord God made a woman from the rib he had taken out of the man, and he brought her to the man." So, dear lady, you see that the male needed someone to whom to give his love, and so God created the female from the male's body. The word *rib* in Genesis 2:22 is the Hebrew word *tsela*. It does not necessarily mean a rib as we understand the word. It can mean either "side" or "chamber." In any event, Scripture is telling us that God drew the woman from a part of the man. Why? Because the receiver has to be exactly like the giver.

Just as man needed to be spirit to receive love from God and be in a relationship with Him, the woman needed to be of the same essence as man to receive love from him. I hope you will begin to appreciate and celebrate your uniqueness, whatever your personality type or culture, especially after reading this last chapter.

Growing up, I was taught to be strong and not soft because being soft meant you were weak and a pushover. This meant behaving like a boy, but that's not how God created a woman to be. God created the woman not to be like the man but to own her identity as a woman.

When God designed the female, He obviously had influence in mind. A woman is a receiver. God designed her to receive from the male and to incubate what she receives so that it can grow and develop. A woman is built to influence. Her wombs—physical, emotional, and mental or spiritual—tremendously influence what they receive by providing a nurturing and transforming environment. There is much truth in the saying, "The hand that rocks the cradle rules the world." Positional power and influence power are not mutually exclusive; they are meant to be exercised together in dominion.

Abraham needed Sarah to help him fulfill his calling. Influence power manifests itself in a very different way. First, a woman may have a title, but she doesn't need a title to lead. She leads by influence. This is why women usually run households. Men call themselves "the head of the house," but it is usually the woman who runs the home.

Second, a woman doesn't need to talk to run things. She leads just by her influence. My dad used to run our household with his mouth. He would say, "Clean the kitchen" or "Take your feet off that chair." However, just one look from my mother had me taking my feet off that chair. The woman doesn't need to say a word; she just looks, and people respond. This is a powerful influence. Some men assume that women are weak because they are quiet or don't bark orders. These people do not understand influence power.

Whatever culture you may come from, you happen to be reading this book, and I am here to provide context from a biblical perspective, which I believe is central. We will look at feminism physically, spiritually and emotionally. A woman has three wombs: the physical womb, the emotional womb, and the mental/spiritual womb.

PHYSICAL FEMININITY

What image comes to your mind first when you think of "a feminine woman"? An hourglass-shaped woman, right? But that's a lie. Over time the enemy, through social media, cultures, and people, has made women believe a lie about their bodies and figures. Different women's bodies are shaped differently. Some are hourglass, apple-shaped, pear-shaped, etc., and guess what? Each shape is beautiful and feminine.

What are the things about your physical appearance that you think you do not like? What things about your body have people consistently told you are wrong? It could be your nose, ears, eyes, legs, etc. Permit me to say that those things are designed perfectly for you. You are perfect as you are; you only need to find what fits you and the body God has given you. Learn your body type and coloring and what lines and colors suit them. Then you can dress in a way that complements your unique self, enabling you to carry yourself with grace and self-love. That is femininity in the physical.

EMOTIONAL FEMININITY

On the emotional level, as a feminine woman, you must learn to first pour into yourself. You truly cannot give what you don't have. Also, the way others treat you will be the reflection of the way you treat yourself. So, dear lady, love yourself unconditionally before expecting love from others.

What is unconditional love? Unconditional love is love without terms and conditions. That doesn't mean it is a love without accountability but rather a love that recognizes you are a unique, fearfully and wonderfully made woman. Practicing this kind of love on yourself is what will enable you to extend that level of tolerance in your relationships. If you accept your own imperfections, then you will be more understanding of the imperfections of others. If you learn from your own lessons, then you create room for others to learn and grow around you.

Why is this continual work on ourselves important? Because in marriage, most couples don't have "relationship problems"; they have problems they bring into the relationship. Your relationship's health starts with the relationship you have with yourself. As women, we must love ourselves in every sense of the word. We work hard, take care of everybody, and hold a lot of responsibility in the world. In that same measure we must love ourselves.

Let me share with you a few of my favorite techniques for learning to give all the big love you give out to others back to yourself. I incorporate these into my morning routine and sometimes during my night routine or my other routines, but please feel free to do them however you like.

1. Keep a journal of the compliments you receive. When you go back and read the nice things people had to say about you at the end of the week or month, you'll be pleasantly surprised by the list you've compiled. The purpose of this list is to shine your mental spotlight on the positive learning to help you accept compliments and speak positively about your body. Words are powerful; your self-talk is extremely important in building your self-worth and enhancing your femininity. It releases grace and confidence. There is the inner child in every human, and your subconscious doesn't know the difference between lies and truth. Whatever you say to your subconscious is what it will believe as your truth. Speaking kindly to yourself and not being overly critical of yourself enhances your feminine grace. The focus here is not to require validation or place a higher value on what others say to you than on what you think of yourself. Rather, it is to appreciate that people give you flowers daily. It's okay to smell them.

2. Speak softly to yourself. Speaking softly is a grace that many ladies have forgotten. We may feel we have to be brazen and harsh to get our points across to others, but this is not the case. We lose our femininity when we do this. Thankfully, it is not too late to change. You can begin now to make changes. Begin with the people in your circle by being soft and sweet. It's an endearing quality for a woman. I recall the Lord teaching me to be soft and sweet. Then in my marriage, it took me literally being intentional

daily, and I learned to even adjust the tone of my voice when speaking with and to my husband, daily doing the little things that would give him joy and that he would appreciate. It wasn't one-sided, of course, as he also made adjustments, and our relationship became so much better. Marriage is a two-way street; the goal is a win–win.

Cultivate sweetness and softness one day at a time. As a DISC Consultant, I understand that there are different personality types, so being sweet and soft may come naturally to some more than others, and that's also okay. You can cultivate being soft and sweet by being intentional, especially if you consider yourself to be someone who speaks and acts roughly or if the people in your life (family and friends) comment on how rough you are. Now is the time to begin to work on being less irritable and more pleasant rather than a boss lady.

3.   Use affirmations. Have you ever looked at yourself in the mirror and said to yourself; "I love you. Wow. There is no one else on the planet like you." You may feel weird doing this, but it is critically important. It allows you to hear someone (you!) tell you those words out loud. So, when you do hear "I love you" from someone else, you're not surprised, you're not in denial, and you actually believe it. The more you say this to yourself, the more you will soon recognize how much people start saying it to you. If you don't believe me, try it. Plant the seed of self-love, water it daily, and watch it grow in your life.

In a journalling exercise in my Ladies in Waiting Masterclass, I encourage each lady to write a letter to her five-year-old self and a letter to her teenage self. These activities heal the inner child and address certain wounds and hurts that have stayed covered and untreated over the years. Get therapy if you need to, but please heal before you get into marriage . . . so that you can have the home of your dreams.

4.   Fill your love tank every day. What do you do that makes you feel recharged and rejuvenated? Make a list of the things that make

you feel good. Keep this list somewhere you'll see it daily, and commit to doing at least one act every day. Here are my top five:

- Exercising daily
- Soaking in a bubble bath at least once a week
- Having wholesome conversations with a friend
- Meditating
- Listening to music
- Using sugar scrub to exfoliate my skin at least once a week

Create your own list and use it regularly, and you'll be pleasantly surprised by how loved you will feel doing this for yourself and how much grace and femininity you will exude just by pouring into your love tank.

5. Affirm another person. Life operates on fundamental laws that are non-negotiable. Life is a boomerang—the more energy you give to something, the more of it you will receive in return. If you want more love, start focusing on the loving aspects of everyone around you and affirming those aspects in people as often as you can. Just know the opposite of this is also true. The more energy you give to negativity, the more negativity you will see. If, for example, you are trolling people on social media, you are engaging in low-vibrational behavior that high-value people have no time for. Be so invested in your personal development and growth that you have no time for drama, gossip, or any habits that don't move you forward toward your destiny.

Many ladies argue that the man must treat them right first. Dear lady, if you don't pour into yourself, how will you recognize counterfeit when it comes along? If you do not learn to respect yourself and value yourself, you will find it difficult to make adjustments and be sweet to your husband. It's important to understand that your husband can be your brother and friend, but he is also your priest and king. And he deserves that honor from you. I encourage ladies, if you know you cannot submit to a man, please don't marry him. Submission should be mutual.

SPIRITUAL FEMININITY

Now let's look at spiritual femininity. Please understand that a woman is unique because she has a spirit inside that makes her a free and responsible spiritual being. Spiritually, men and women are equal; they have the same spirit man within. God called both male and female "man." The Word of God expresses it in Galatians 3:28 (NIV): "There is neither . . . slave nor free, nor is there male and female, for you are all one in Christ Jesus." First Peter 3:4 (NIV) says that a woman's beauty "should be that of [her] inner self, the unfading beauty of a gentle and quiet spirit, which is of great worth in God's sight." It is this "inner self" that is a woman's spirit. The physical woman is different from what she is in her inner self. The spirit man inside every woman is the being that relates to God.

Dear lady, the next time you meet someone who is confused about this concept, just tell them, "Look, I have a female body, but I have a spirit man inside. I'm female because of what I have to do physically and in God's kingdom on the planet; however, I deal directly with God as a spirit." Jesus said, "God is spirit, and his worshipers must worship in the Spirit and in truth" (John 4:24 NIV). A woman has her own spirit being with which to worship God. She can bless the Lord, love the Lord, and receive from the Lord herself. A woman can preach, not because she's female, but because she has a spirit man within her.

Because a spirit man lives within the woman, the man's treatment of the woman must be taken very seriously. God honors and respects the woman. He loves and identifies with the spirit man inside the female, and so He takes special care in regard to her. When you offend the spirit man, you offend God.

Dear lady, learn to fill your tank by soaking yourself in worship; this brings healing and wholeness to your spirit. For a woman who prays a lot or engages in spiritual warfare, spending time to soak in worship opens the portal of the spirit and opens a woman to her feminine grace.

When you stop searching for "the one" and start identifying yourself as "the one"—loving yourself in the way you've longed to be loved and embracing your very own wholeness as an independent living and breathing being—you become the love you'll attract. You are enough. That is the key to not settling in love.

Femininity is powerful, and when you find a woman who has learned to walk in her identity and grace as a feminine woman, she becomes a walking powerhouse that births glory and grace and, most importantly, becomes irresistible. Unfortunately, many ungodly women use their femininity to seduce men and break homes because many godly women have not learned to embrace and walk in their identity as feminine women. That is why I want you, the woman reading this book, to embrace your femininity.

Reflection

Do you find yourself easily irritable? Or have you lost your feminine grace due to the environment in which you find yourself or because you had a difficult childhood? That's okay. There are things out of our control and things within our control. You can begin to make changes one step at a time. Become intentional with the changes you want to make. A masculine man doesn't want a masculine woman. They repel. So, as you prepare yourself for your marriage, love you, build you, and become the delectable and beautiful woman you were created to be. I believe every woman is beautiful.

Conclusion

As I end this book, I want you to know I believe in you, and I believe in your authenticity and your story. Keep winning.

If this book has blessed you and if you have learned a thing or two from it, please pass it on. Get a copy for one or more of the people in your life, and let us build a company of women who know their worth and are prepared with the right resources and information on marriage.

Please feel free to reach out to me by email to share your journey. I look forward to connecting and hearing from you.

Email: deborahacademyhq@gmail.com
Website: www.deborahacademy.com
Instagram: https://www.instagram.com/debsidowuasufi/
Facebook: https://www.facebook.com/deborah.nnadiekwe
LinkedIn: https://www.linkedin.com/in/deborah-idowu-asufi-7ab2442b9/

The Ladies in Waiting Masterclass

Allow me to introduce you to the Ladies in Waiting Masterclass. This masterclass is for you if:

- You are a single lady who deeply desires to have a kingdom marriage but does not know how to become a kingdom lady or even how to attract the right kingdom man. People say good men are a thing of the past, but that's NOT true. God still has his sons worldwide and they can find you too.
- You want a better marriage than your parents had, a marriage better than what you saw growing up, or even a marriage better than the marriages around you.
- You experienced trauma or any form of abuse and emotional wounds in any season of your life, childhood or adulthood, or you experienced abuse in your past relationships and you desire to heal from it. According to statistics, people who get into marriage with unhealed emotional wounds or abuse of any kind and unhealed traumas end up in divorce or frustrate themselves and their partners in the marriage.
- You have noticed a negative family pattern of untimely death, divorce, broken marriages, women assuming the role of the man in the marriage, etc., and you don't want that to happen in your own marriage.
- You experience marital disappointment and marital delay even though you are beautiful, smart, intelligent, caring, etc.
- Most of the men who are drawn to you are wrong for you.
- You want to know how to position yourself right to meet the husband of your dreams.

- You know a godly home is possible, and you want to know how to build one.
- You want to be a wholesome woman who knows her purpose and is walking in it.

The Ladies in Waiting Masterclass is a course specifically designed to transform your life and make your unmarried years super fulfilling, rather than just waiting for a husband to come.

Past participants have gotten all of the following from the Ladies in Waiting Masterclass:

- **Self-discovery.** You become a wholesome and elegant woman living her best life, thoroughly refined and transformed, managing life's pressure and making informed decisions on marriage from a place of self-discovery. You move from emotionally broken and wounded to emotionally healed and confident.
- **Community.** You will find a community of like minds (other kingdom ladies and me, your coach) that will hold your hands as you journey through life and heal from past wounds. Iron sharpens iron. So, you will be sharpened and challenged to know you and to be you.
- **Freedom from negative influences.** You learn how to be freed from powers or curses that may be keeping your marriage from manifesting.
- **Knowledge.** You become mentally, spiritually, and financially ready to begin a kingdom marriage.

What's included in the Ladies in Waiting Masterclass?

- 12 transformational weeks of group coaching
- 11 modules of teachings and strategy sessions
- Two 60-minute group calls (recording/replay available)
- A 24/7 course community for interaction and reinforced learning

- Uncommon, strategic, targeted, and breakthrough prayer sessions that deal with delays, obstacles, hindrances, and oppositions

Bonus: **50 Questions to Ask During Courtship.** During courtship, essential questions often are not asked, either because they are unknown or because they have been forgotten due to the honeymoon phase of love and red flags ignored. These questions give you focus and perspective.

WHAT WE COVER OVER THE TWELVE WEEKS

Module 1: Trauma, emotional wounds and abuse and your emotional responses to events in your life. Some ladies do not even acknowledge they are dealing with an emotional baggage . . . because they are not self-aware.

Module 2: Processing wounds from your past. How have you handled these? And what is the best way to handle them?

Module 3: Foundations. Have you looked at your Foundation? Do you even know you have one? We explore this in depth.

Module 4: Uncovering negative family patterns. Here we focus on how to identify evil programming from family patterns.

Module 5: Breaking free from negative family patterns. Here we focus on how to break free from evil foundations. Some ladies are still casualties, and they do not know why. Beautiful, intelligent, smart women keep experiencing failed relationships, strange dreams, and strange encounters even after giving their lives to Christ.

Module 6: Self-discovery. How to find you.

Module 7: Valuing the authentic you. Developing soft skills and executive skills.

Module 8: Knowing your Lord and loving Him.

Module 9: We deal in depth with actually walking with God as a woman—not simply church attendance, but the real deal.

Module 10: Finding the right man. We learn and unlearn strategies here, and we also dig up red flags.

Module 11: Nurturing your relationship to marriage. Learn strategies for how to build, what to say and what not to say, and how to navigate this pivotal phase—the phase when many ladies overlook issues that will have them crying later.

WHAT PAST PARTICIPANTS SAY ABOUT THIS COURSE

"One of the most resonant revelations from this course is the renewed perspective on marriage. The belief in a God-ordained marriage, where two complete beings come together to complement and support each other, resonates deeply within me. Marriage is truly beautiful and I can have a God-ordained marriage with one of God's sons!"
—**Priscilla E.**

"Okay, it's sad, no more Friday prayer nights after today. Prayer nights were one of my highlights during the course. I learned to pray a lot, important prayers that I really needed. All I can say is that I wish this course was offered to me 10-15 years ago, I could have saved myself a lot of dating headaches and heartbreak and vice versa. I have learned, relearned and learned a lot of things. Personally, I truly enjoyed how the course was structured; we started with past wounds. This was key; in order for me to be the better version of me, I needed to visit my past and seek healing, for there is a balm in Gilead. I really want to take my time and go over the classes again. All I can say is thank you. I think I made my book reviews longer and longer. A lot I would love to cover was already covered in my book reviews hence, I will end here by saying thank you."
—**Ms. Achieng O**

"Reflecting on the past 12 weeks, I find myself wavering between overwhelming gratitude and a sense of profound self-discovery. This course has been a beacon of light, illuminating the corners of my emotional landscape, fostering emotional healing, and nurturing emotional intelligence. The foundational deliverance from family patterns and delays has been nothing short of liberating, as I have gained insight into generational influences that had long remained hidden. This newfound awareness, rather than daunting, empowers me with the knowledge that my narrative can be rewritten, just as Mary Magdalene was transformed by the presence of Jesus. The selection of resources and books was a treasure trove of wisdom. The authors' ability to articulate the shared experiences of women resonated deeply with me. Their insights served as both mirrors reflecting my journey and guideposts pointing the way forward."

—Ms. Blessing E.

"My 12-week LADIES IN WAITING journey has been nothing short of transformative. I have emerged from it with a deeper connection to God, a greater understanding of myself, and a sense of healing and wholeness that I didn't think was possible. This journey has reaffirmed my faith in God's love and grace and has shown me that with Him, I can overcome any challenge. I am immensely grateful for this experience and look forward to continuing my journey of growth and healing with God by my side. And as I reflect on these 12 weeks, I am filled with gratitude for the transformative power of faith-based therapy, we need this in every nation, this is more than therapy, and you can't do therapy without Jesus. I have emerged from this journey with a deeper understanding of myself, a renewed relationship with God, and a sense of purpose. I have learned that healing is an ongoing process, and I am now equipped with the tools to continue this journey of self-discovery and spiritual growth. My story is one of transformation, and I am excited to embrace the future with faith, hope, and a heart full of gratitude. My mentality has changed; I have learned, unlearned, and relearned. I'm worth it, and yea while I'm still working on myself, with what I've learned, with God on my side and proper mentorship, I now know what to look out for in a man, and I'm pretty sure I'll do well in my marriage. Not just well, I'll do exceedingly well, and God will be proud of me. I'm going to make a good wife. I'm still learning, and I won't stop being better. Once again, thank you, mama, for answering the call; you've been a blessing to me."

—Ms. Joy T.

Are you still wondering if this course is for you? Wonder no more . . . you are about to get a life transformation.

For more information or to register, visit **www.deborahacademy.com**

MEET YOUR COACH

Just like many church girls, I, Deborah Idowu-Asufi, had my dreams about living happily ever after. Yet for many years, they were not being fulfilled. I understood the expectations of friends and family about my marriage. but I was more concerned about my own expectations. It was low-key worrying and challenging that I had not yet found a husband. I understand the fears, pains, dreams and hopes of the unmarried Christian lady. I've been there and I've done that. I also have walked with many unmarried ladies who are now married, and I resonate with their hopes, dreams, aspirations, and joys.

So, I will be honored if you would let me hold your hand, and let's walk this journey to wholeness together. Isolation is the thief of fulfillment. God did not intend for us to journey through life alone. Join this community of intentional women to walk into wholeness and live your best life.

Many married women wish they'd known half of what this course offers and had the opportunity to make an informed choice of partner. So, if you actually follow the teachings and all the course entails, you will have your evidence.

Looking forward to seeing you on the other side. What are you still waiting for? Register or learn more at www.deborahacademy.com.

The Clarity Bootcamp

The Clarity Bootcamp is designed to help you to re-discover yourself and your identity.

This Bootcamp is for you if:

- You have a project, assignment, vision, business, ministry, NGO, etc., that you are sitting on and have not executed yet due to varying reasons, maybe fear, uncertainty, imposter syndrome, feelings of inadequacy, or general inertia.
- You have an entrepreneurial spirit and you are a proactive, highly motivated self-starter who wants to walk with purposeful women with like minds and core values such as discipline, accountability, honor, integrity, determination, passion, courage, consistency, attitude, effort, and perseverance.
- You are in a season where there is a restlessness on your inside because even though you are doing great according to the standards and in the eyes of other people, deep down you know there is more to you than meets the eye.
- You want to be *all* you were created to be and do. You do not want to look back at your life and wish you had done this or that, or that you missed an opportunity. You want to max out your potential.
- You desire clarity to walk in the blueprint of your current season. Many people know what to do but lack the desired clarity on the "how."
- Your unique gifts and skills are unquestionable, but your results do not reflect them.

- You are aware there are destinies attached to you, and you seek a fuller expression of your purpose and destiny.
- You are a Kingmaker, walking in positions of authority, you have years of experience, and you have honed your skills, and you want to use all you have to make a difference in your world, to bring God glory, and to transform lives, families, and generations yet unborn.
- Fulfillment is at the core of all you do, and you want to decisively and intentionally pursue purpose with an inner circle or tribe that walks the talk with integrity and excellence.
- You are a leader with striking and undeniable executive attention to detail, and you know how to make things happen for yourself and others.

If you are ready to take charge of your life, enjoy clarity, and take on new territories, visit deborahacademy.com to learn more about Clarity Bootcamp and register.

About the Author

Deborah Idowu-Asufi is an international speaker, transformative leader, global advocate, and mentor renowned for empowering women to embrace their unique identity and walk boldly in their God-ordained purpose. Giving her heart to the Lord at the age of 15, Deborah's unwavering love for God has guided her through life's challenges and inspired countless others to do the same.

A passionate advocate for women's empowerment, Deborah has addressed prestigious platforms such as the United Nations Annual Women Event in New York (2024), where she spoke on gender equality and equipping women to rise above societal limitations.

As the founder of the Ladies in Waiting Masterclass, Deborah has mentored hundreds of single women, helping them discover their purpose, make informed decisions, and position themselves for Kingdom marriages. Her teachings redefine singleness as a season of growth and self-discovery, empowering women to thrive in this unique phase of life.

With over two decades of mentorship, Deborah has impacted thousands of women globally, guiding them to uncover their "superpowers," build confidence, and align with God's best for their lives. Many of her mentees are now thriving in their purpose and enjoying fulfilling Kingdom marriages.

An accomplished scholar and professional, Deborah holds a Diploma in Insurance and Risk Management, a BA in History and Diplomatic

Studies, and a Master's in International Affairs and Diplomacy. She is also a Board-Certified Financial Professional, seamlessly blending academic excellence with ethical, principle-based coaching.

Her influence extends beyond women's empowerment. As the founder of Deborah Academy, a 21st-century institution for cultivating professionals and business leaders, and The Transformation Commission, an NGO with a global impact across Nigeria, the UK, USA, Canada, and Australia, Deborah has helped countless individuals create meaningful success and impact.

Deborah's faith-centered approach ensures every individual she mentors experiences transformation, clarity, and empowerment. Known for her sweet spirit and powerful presence, she inspires others to rise above challenges, embrace their uniqueness, and live fully in their God-given identity.

Deborah Idowu-Asufi is not just a coach, mentor, and speaker—she is a catalyst for change, a visionary author, and a global voice of transformation. Her life's work is a testament to her belief that when women discover their uniqueness and align with their purpose, they become unstoppable forces of influence and light.

www.ingramcontent.com/pod-product-compliance
Lightning Source LLC
Chambersburg PA
CBHW070752120626
46557CB00002B/565